REFLECTIONS OF GLADNESS

Editorial/Press Supervision & Design: Karan Sheets

The author and publisher express their appreciation to the following for permission to include the following material.

Photographs courtesy of the Edgar Cayce Foundation where indicated.
Jim Hayden and Debbie Strole for "13 Violets for Miss Gladys,"
    photos by Karan Sheets.
William Kluge for the front cover photography.
Karan Sheets for graphic elements and nature photography.
T.J. Davis for permission to use the photograph of Edgar Cayce's hat and
    photographs from the personal album of Gladys Davis Turner.
Persian Horse used in photo-composite by Karan Sheets,
    courtesy of Miho Museum, Kyoto, Japan.
Newspaper clippings from Helen Crist, "A Half Century Tribute Is Paid
    For Dedication." *The Beacon,* September 27, 1973, 14-15.

Library of Congress Cataloging-in-Publication Data

Kluge, Micki
    Reflections of Gladness : Edgar Cayce's vision of the Work shared in a collection of
    memories of Gladys Davis / Micki Kluge.
    ISBN: 978-0-578-08504-3
    Spiritual Life-Reincarnation.

Cato Douglas
Virginia Beach, Virginia

1st edition, May, 2011
Printed in the United States of America

REFLECTIONS OF GLADNESS

EDGAR CAYCE'S

vision of the Work shared in
a collection of memories of

GLADYS DAVIS

by MICKI KLUGE

Cato Douglas

GLADYS DAVIS

IN GLADITUDE

In our tribute in memory of Dorothy Gladys Davis Turner Wilmore, we recognize her title as given by the Herald Angel who announced in her mother's dream, "Her name is to be GLADNESS!" Witnesses of her nature acclaimed the match of her soul's proclamation.

Edgar Cayce was introduced to the world as a twentieth century prophet, psychic healer and spiritual seer extraordinaire. Truth seekers, pursuing their "Master's" degrees in applying their study of his map, probably learned of his expert cartography in their "Search for God." Gladys recorded his recommended routes.

With this collection of recent reflections, we wish to express our profound appreciation for the dedicated life of Mr. Cayce's twin soul who exemplified the unique value of his expertise. As a devoted guardian, Gladys recorded and preserved the archives of the sketches he logged during his lifetime and the traces he reproduced from past eons.

On behalf of all whose lives have been enhanced through awareness of Edgar Cayce as God's twentieth century Messenger, we share her essence of Gladness. For those of us who did not know Edgar Cayce personally, she acted in the role of his representative, as an emissary seeking no acclaim for her own essential contributions to their joint life mission. In her exemplary humility as his scribe and record keeper, no one could have honored Mr. Cayce with greater respect, or served with greater dependability in their joint mission tasks.

Edgar Cayce was born for the special service of aiding humanity to discover its individual seeds of Spiritual Purpose, implanted within each soul incarnated on this beautiful planet. In his struggle to fulfill his own sense of purpose, God granted him assistance in magnifying his rare talents. He was blessed with an ideal wife, Gertrude Evans, and two devoted sons, Hugh Lynn and Edgar Evans Cayce, each uniquely endowed to share his mission of Enlightenment with the world. Thanks to his last clairvoyant letter to the Board of Trustees, Gladys continued to stand in his behalf, assuring the permanence of reputable records, consistent with the literal usage of his words as expressed by the Source of Wisdom. She honored their accuracy, knowing that understanding would come in response to the integrity of the seeker.

As author of Edgar Cayce's first biography, *"There Is A River,"* Thomas Sugrue introduced a thoroughly comprehensive approach to the psychic healer, the prophet's mission in twentieth century America and the world at large. We share Tom's sentiments for Edgar Cayce and appreciation for the secretary with whom he shared their mutual admiration. His poem aptly describes Gladys as she is pictured in this book, sitting on the ledge of the steps leading into the library of the Cayce home headquarters with this birthday greeting:

For Gladys: At Twenty-Nine

How sweet to be just twenty–nine!
The grapes of youth have turned to wine,
And nature's finished her design
(All except the valentine).
The sun is used to kissing you,
And lots of men are waiting to.
Every violet knows your laughter;
Mice adore you from the rafter,
Everybody tells each other;
Mouse tells man and man tells brother;
Trees tell roots and roots tell earth;
Just how much they think you're worth.
And the price is very odd
(For who can value things of God?)
"Gladys: Made of solid gold;
Keep until she's very old.
Use with caution; do not waste;
Rare: Can never be replaced."

by Tom Sugrue

FOREWORD

In the calm and stillness, a true reflection appears, mirroring its source with clarity and depth. Rarely in life do we witness souls who so clearly glow with an aura of beauty and love that our lives are forever colored with their impressions. Through these pages runs a golden thread; one of connectivity, faith, trust and love where far-flung souls come together through time and space to bring glad tidings to those of us who seek God's Face in all things. It is an amazing story, a fabric richly woven of past lives, tragic fates, brilliant flashes of victory, dark days of the soul and enduring faithfulness spanning eons in our pursuit of Truth and Light.

Tom Sugrue, author of "*There Is A River*," a book which has introduced so many to the life and work of Edgar Cayce, clearly perceived the impact of the soft-spoken Cayce and his Work in his 1943 letter to David Kahn.

> It is a love story, too, in all of love's manifestations and nuances: love of a good woman, love of home and family, love of country, love of God, love of truth, love of integrity.
>
> But I would think that reincarnation could be left aside and a simple, homespun document of a man serving God in a way not familiar to the people could be made of this heart-breaking story. In Hopkinsville, before the bearded doctors in Bowling Green, in Selma, in Texas, in Dayton, at Virginia Beach—readings are given, and the pitiful things: the lame, the halt, the blind—see, walk and live. Yet the eyes of the multitude are turned away, unbelieving.
>
> It is, you see, a great PARABLE, a great ALLEGORY, for our times: our age of skepticism, rejecting faith, rejecting God, rejecting miracles, rejecting His Sign.
> [R6-254-113]

The lives of Edgar Cayce and Gladys Davis reveal that true love story, but not the kind you might think. Described as "twin souls" throughout Cayce's psychic Readings, they were united in vision and purpose, entering the earth through not one, but many lifetimes. Twin souls work together in "a realm of knowledge, or a realm of understanding ... for these are one when they are turned in the same direction." [538-59] The concept of twin souls differs from that of our familiar term, "soul mates." While soul mates serve to complement each other through romantic relationships, twin souls unite in spirit forces to pursue joint endeavors outside themselves.

The Readings reveal the soul mission of Edgar Cayce existed even before man appeared in the earth.

> ... we find in the beginning, when the first elements were given, and the forces set in motion that brought about the sphere as we find called earth plane, and when the morning stars sang together, and the whispering winds brought the news of the coming of man's indwelling, of the spirit of the Creator, became the living soul. This entity came into being with this multitude. [294-8]

These two have ever been together, you see... Each time this entity [Gladys Davis]... has been in the earth plane with the entity [Edgar Cayce]. [294-9]

We find these, as in the present earth's plane, have had many experiences together, and their soul and spirit are well-knit, and must of necessity present each that they may be one. For we find in the beginning, that they ... were as one in mind, soul, spirit, body; and in the first earth's plane as the voice over many waters, when the glory of the Father's giving of the earth's indwelling of man was both male and female in one. [288-6]

Through the experiences of their lives, we glimpse a vista broader than our ability to comprehend; one where, through Infinite Grace and Mercy, we are allowed to enter the earth again and again to grow and mature in our awareness of our relationship to our Creator and the splendor of His Creation. When we think of reincarnation, often we consider our own lifetimes and their effect on our spiritual progress. Here, we see beyond to a world where many souls are drawn to unite in purpose to help others realize we are One in spirit.

In this they are again united in soul and in spirit forces, and through the joy and the pleasure of selfless service they may again know the meaning of these as given.

They need only remain in the future faithful one to the other, ever giving, ever retaining those joys of the relations that bring and give of self in service to others; and these bring joy, peace, and again uniting of body, soul and spirit in the next. Remain faithful, therefore, unto the end; gaining those joys through daily acts of selflessness for and with others, remembering that in these manifestations they (and all souls) become knit one with the other. [288-6]

Together, they—with Edgar Cayce's family and the "Glad Helpers" who joined them—developed a powerhouse of knowledge spanning health, reincarnation, future prophecy, ancient mysteries, the lifetimes of Jesus, our relationship with God and with each other. The realm of souls does not conform to a hierarchical model; rather, it resembles more the galaxies of our universe, thousands of beacons of light interwoven through time and experience, drawn together by the unifying force of the Source, our Creator.

This is also the story of two dear friends, Gladys Davis and Micki Kluge. By choosing to write this book in her honor, Micki affords us the rare pleasure of getting to know Gladys through the eyes of those who knew and cherished her. Cayce, himself, would revel in its contents as he, too, instantly recognized the gem that was Gladys. In her first Reading, he astutely outlined her nature.

> Goodly soul, and rather old, you see. One destined to bring, both from its own self and from the experiences of the past, much good to many peoples, and much good for individuals who put their trust and faith in the entity, for the soul and spirit of this entity has seen many and various phases of the evolution of the human family.
> One who, with others, will draw much of the more beautiful things of the earth plane about them, and one to whom obstacles become the stepping stones for higher development in this present earth plane. [288-1]

When they first met in this lifetime, Micki recognized Gladys as the little girl she had loved during her life in ancient Egypt. The soul recognition was mutual, as Gladys reunited with her friend of centuries past. Together, they embarked on their journey through this experience, each providing the other with joyous affection and plentiful laughter, renewing bonds which survive life itself.

Rarely are we blessed with an awareness of our past associations. At the end of our days, we may reflect back on those we've known and how events have shaped our lives. So, it is with past lives for the spiritually adept; we recognize those we've known before like old friends we haven't seen in many years. The roles, costumes and settings change, but the bonds remain. The gift of recall can also be a two-edged sword, recalling past challenges and downfalls. We are reminded we must take up our stories where they left off before, until we can with compassion forgive and seek redemption, thus closing the karmic door left open by past transgressions.

Throughout this work appear images of birds, flowers and butterflies which brought delight to the gentle spirit that was Gladness, Gladys Davis. They represent our tribute to her happy nature and reflect our best and loving wishes for her spirit's journey. She gathered beauty around her like a resplendent robe, embracing Nature's gifts, cooing babies, weddings and birthdays with radiance and laughter. She was not one to seek fame or fortune, living a life so simple and lean, few could imagine. Half her earnings supported her extended family, a quarter went to Mrs. Cayce for room and board, leaving scarce resources for her own enjoyment. Yet the humble spirit of this beautiful woman has touched the lives of millions. Edgar Cayce's work would have been known to only the few who requested his aid if it weren't for the tenacity and endurance of Gladys Davis, the Guardian at the gate, the Protector of the Readings, the strong, resilient "Gladitude" which bolstered the spirits of others when all was thought to be lost.

Saint Therese of Lisieux, in "Story of a Soul," so beautifully writes:

> Jesus set before me the book of nature. I understand how all the flowers God has created are beautiful, how the splendor of the rose and the whiteness of the lily do not take away from the perfume of the violet or the delightful simplicity of the daisy. I understand that if all flowers wanted to be roses, nature would lose her springtime beauty, and the fields would no longer be decked out with little wild flowers. So it is in the world of souls, Jesus' garden. He has created smaller ones and those must be content to be daisies or violets destined to give joy to God's glances when He looks down at His feet. Perfection consists in doing His will, in being what He wills us to be.

Prepare to enter a land where giant angels walk among us, where soft-spoken Southern drawls spelled out mysteries beyond our imagination. One could not ask for a better friend or companion along the way than Gladys Davis. She joined her twin soul, Edgar Cayce, as they dedicated their lives to bring us this message:

> Use that thou hast in hand today ... unto the glory of God and not of self, and tomorrow those things necessary to be done are shown thee. Dost thou want to tell God how to use thee? Let God use thee as HE sees fit! Dost thou choose to tell thine neighbor as to how he should serve God? Rather shouldn't thou choose to ask God to USE thy neighbor, with THINE help, as GOD sees fit—and not as THOU seest fit? This was the rebellion in heaven, and is the rebellion in the soul of man—telling God what to do with His Own! [288-36]

Take this thou hast in hand and make and mold it into the present plane's development, that thyself and others may know that God is God, and demands of His creatures that of the knowledge of self, that they may better serve their fellows ... bringing others to the knowledge of Him. [294-8]

As ye study to show thyself approved unto God, a workman not ashamed, rightly dividing the words of truth and keeping self unspotted from the world, it will come into thy experience—and ye shall know it ... [2023-1]

So, into that bright light of awareness we step, shedding the narrow views of the past, grateful to share the joy of our salvation in the discovery of the uplifting spirit of Truth. Thank you, Micki, for opening the door to the welcome sanctuary of Gladness and letting us learn to embrace her as you did, a friend for all the ages to come.

PREFACE

Presenting viewpoints of Edgar Cayce's twin soul, Gladys Davis Turner Wilmore, Executive Secretary, Archivist and Mentor from the perspective of her friends, family, peers and avid followers, we share a variety of "Reflections" of her brilliance in the services she performed while promoting their healing mission for humanity.

The value of Reincarnation as a tool in developing our mutual use of Christ Consciousness evolves through our study and application of the Research and Enlightenment they taught by example for our Association of members in the search for Truth in seeking understanding of our relationships with God and mankind.

We honor Gladys Davis as an ideal Reflection of one whose application of major tenets of Edgar Cayce's legacy exhibits humanity's attunement to God. Her surviving associates were invited to contribute their memories and evaluations to create an anthology exemplifying her remarkable service. In addition I have inserted numerous personal anecdotes, reflecting their joint influences on my personal and general philosophy during the decades of our mutual friendship. Linking our relationship through the eons of ongoing reincarnation with many of the same entities that peopled those associations throughout our shared history inspires soliloquies, as my reveries usurp the spotlight which Gladys always adeptly evaded. Yet, her own fluency could soar when she explained the ineffable, as Edgar Cayce's Readings often testify.

This collection of memories has synthesized into a monocle-peephole for a personal glimpse into a panoramic landscape where giants presided. With the attitude of "Gladitude," my appreciation extends to these contributors whose own reflections inspire followers who continue the Work of Edgar Cayce's enlightenment, which she served to expand so devotedly.

In sharing memories of her with our mutual friend, Barbara Robinson, of Tucson, AZ, I was encouraged to write about her various contributions to that pool of wisdom which reflects her image. Alert to the growing hunger in our world for inspirational guidance, Barbara, urged me to display more details of Gladys' personal legacy with the beneficiaries of their ordained mission. Believing that these are little known, or unpublished, vignettes of her life which may be of interest to others, we hope the collection endears to you her sterling nature as the wholesome friend we knew.

Because Barbara Robinson, and her husband, Lytle, were vitally involved during the early years of founding the Association for Research and Enlightenment (A.R.E.) it seems fitting to open this celebration of Gladness with Barbara's own beautiful tribute to Gladys entitled:

"Thoughts On Gladys"

"The Cayce phenomenon seems to be another major move on the part of the Creator, in His infinite wisdom and love, to tell us the truth that will set us free."
To quote: Robert L. Smock, THE SEARCHLIGHT, July '59

Those of us who accept that Edgar Cayce has truly been used by God to provide spiritual enlightenment welcome the opportunity of honoring Gladys Davis who devoted her life to recording, preserving and promoting that valuable information.

As to personal contact with Gladys, since our family did not live at Virginia Beach, I only had the opportunity of being with her a few times. When my husband, Lytle, and I first met her in the early 1950s, I recall vividly how excited she was that a portion of the Readings had been catalogued by subject. Gladys was particularly anxious for the Cayce material to become broadly circulated nationwide. When she learned that my husband was a writer, she put aside all other commitments to search for information he needed to complete a series of articles centering on the Cayce Readings. This effort on her part continued over a period of many years just as it did for numerous other writers. Before the era of computers and copiers, Gladys spent untold hours researching the Readings for writers and corresponding with those who lived out of her area.

We honor this dear lady for being a "valiant pioneer" in the Cayce work which was often ridiculed initially, but Gladys was also part of the foundation of that organization. As most know, with few exceptions, the mass of over 14,000 Cayce Readings were recorded [in shorthand] and typed by her. In early publications circulated to members on various subjects, it was Gladys who extracted information and presented it—often anonymously. Through the years, she taught courses at the annual A.R.E. Congress meetings which drew people from all over the country. She wrote numerous articles and also presented talks at the Headquarters' Sunday Forums which were published in the A.R.E. publication, *THE SEARCHLIGHT,* on various subjects: "Imagery Or Reality?" (Jul '50); "Osteopathy From The Edgar Cayce Readings" (Dec '59); "The Power of Attitudes in Serious Disorders" (Aug '59, Nov '60); "Pharmacology In The Edgar Cayce Readings" (Jan '58); "The Body Is The Temple" (Jul '57); "The Bible And You" (May '57); "Influences From Without" (May '49); "Problems and Their Solutions From the Edgar Cayce Readings" (Feb '61); "The Panorama of Rebirth" (Sep '57); "How Long Is Tomorrow?" (Sep '57); and "Edgar and Gertrude Cayce As I Knew Them" (Sep '64).

Despite her contributions Gladys remained humble and once explained, "You see, he [Cayce] never heard a reading. We got our encouragement from the Readings, but he got his from the results of the Readings which he saw in the lives of those around him. It kept us on our toes, because we knew that if he once saw a harmful effect in our lives from the Readings, he'd stop giving them; and we had gradually gotten so we couldn't live without them." (*THE SEARCHLIGHT,* Sep '64).

Through the years, Gladys remained in awe of Mr. Cayce's psychic ability. She told about one incident which occurred during the six years she took care of her young nephew in their home. One day while she was taking down a reading, she glanced out the window and saw the little boy right at the water's edge of the lake on the property. She recorded, "Mr. Cayce, lying there on the couch with his eyes closed, stopped in the middle of the reading and said, 'Go and get the child.' I ran out and got him, came back and sat down and the reading continued."

Gladys acknowledged the change in her own life as a result of contact with the Readings. "I came to feel that everyone I met was an opportunity for me to understand and work out a relationship. The Readings pointed out that if we have an emotional reaction to a person, either good or bad [whether positive or negative], it is a sign that we have something to work out. Then, the casual meeting of someone in the street, or at the grocery, or on a bus, takes on special meaning. When we begin to think that nothing happens by chance, then every meeting, every activity, takes on special importance ... We are as tiny cogs in the wheel of God's progress."

In my opinion, Gladys, was far more than a "tiny cog." She stands tall as fulfilling a significant and vital role in dispensing the information which came through the Readings of Edgar Cayce. For that, I am grateful and appreciative.

It is extremely difficult to fully grasp or truly comprehend just how far-reaching the positive impact of Gladys Davis' dedicated commitment as a single individual has been on the lives of hundreds of thousands of people around the world during the course of her lifetime, rippling forward through her incarnations from as far back as Atlantis, and what it will be, carrying forward to influence future generations of humanity.

Barbara has summed up Gladys' valuable assets so beautifully. Reflecting the essence of Edgar Cayce's divine Purpose, Gladness expressed his portrait of a Masterpiece.

Together, we envisioned a tribute to a woman of great brilliance—both intellectually and spiritually—whose genuinely compassionate way of living produced a clear path worthy of following. Our lives were richly enhanced by her friendship and example for more than six decades of service to this "Work." Fellow travelers who knew Gladys happily share evidence of mutual reveries and praise, sprouting with potentials of fruit that can nourish those who did not have the privilege of knowing her.

As an octogenarian with a conspicuous lack of technological skills, my efforts toward this project has been flooded by willing helpers. My granddaughter, Alexis Waller, welcomed by Gladys' arms as a fellow Aquarian just hours after her birth, assisted me with my initial interviews. Staff members of the Association for Research and Enlightenment (A.R.E.) have graciously helped make many of our contacts possible. I marvel that Mariana Theos' patience with me is akin to that Gladys exemplified throughout our friendship, "cut from the same bolt of cloth," as my mother may have expressed. Gladys' niece, Karen Davis, is a family bridge of inspiration, reflecting hope from her soul's likeness.

Alexis and I heard many songs of praise for Gladys in the recounting of profound regards. It was greatly encouraging to hear the glowing verbal accolades expressed in our initial phone calls with those who knew her as an indispensable aide in directing their careers and inspiring their own lives. Their glowing sentiments fired our hopes of receiving a wealth of promising reflections to form a meaningful medley, for those who missed the distinct privilege of knowing her as "Gladness," Miss Gladys, Mrs. Turner, Wilmore, or just Gladys Davis.

This has been a wonderful excuse to converse with the dwindling remnant of pioneering souls that knew her who have scattered literally around the globe. Living their own enlightened lives, they are busy spreading the inspiring messages Gladys Davis transcribed from the Source speaking through the Edgar Cayce Readings.

This congenial network of dedicated souls, who have once again entered Earth at this time in human history, are representative alumni of various schools from eons past, singing and dancing to the same unifying music and verse, all wearing distinctive costumes and sporting diverse world views styled to fit each new generation. Heading up this present cavalcade are the outstanding principle figures: Edgar Cayce and Gladys Davis, Gertrude, Hugh Lynn and Edgar Evans Cayce, Tom Sugrue, the Blumenthals, Mildred Davis, Ruth Burks, T.J. Davis and others who repeatedly reappear in the panoramic pageantry of this multi-incarnation epic drama.

In shifting from the initial anthology format envisioned, these personal reminiscences delve more into effects that reincarnation itself has etched through the eons since Edgar Cayce (as RaTa) and Gertrude (as Isis) in Egypt were the parents of "the perfect child" model, Gladys (as Iso) who has become today's model of "Gladness." Her influence shines throughout every angle of my personal viewpoints, though possibly warped by the chinks in my individual looking-glasses. Her tolerance of my imperfections was phenomenal, inspiring my optimism in daring to share them with you.

ACKNOWLEDGEMENTS

Across the eons we have renewed our friendships again and again through the many facets of our lifetimes together. Cooperation inspired by the dedicated service of Gladys Davis is reflected in our mutual commitment to share the values gleaned from spiritual channels of insight, as she and Edgar Cayce pioneered their application throughout their lives and associations. Reflective memories of the generous contributors who knew the "Gladness" she emitted are gratefully shared and submitted as evidence to honor her achievements with the "Work."

In "Gladitude" I list the crew of supporters, A.R.E.'s staff encircling the Globe who linked my connection with her mutual friends, and the assistants of the Edgar Cayce Foundation who provided Archived photos to be added to those from Gladys' family and my own collection. Many thanks as well to the Edgar Cayce Foundation for granting their permission to use extracts of the Readings where appropriate.

Thanks to T. J. Davis for sharing photos from Gladys' personal photo album and scrapbook, as well as his own mementos. Special thanks to Anne Davis and Debbie Strole, Gladys' nieces, for sharing Jim Hayden's painting "13 Violets for Miss Gladys." Jim, your artistry glows with love and beauty.

My sincere appreciation to many encouraging friends and the tolerant support of my family: Ray (enduring sixty years as husband), Karen (our mutual Joy), Bill (our added Bonus), John and Tricia (their perfect partners), plus their special daughters who enhance our lives: Alexis, Casey, Jesse, and Lindsay.

For the expertise of assistants in the realm of 21st century technology who struggled to translate my archaic language from the clay tablets of ancient Sanskrit, my appreciation and admiration is incalculable:

Alexis Garland Waller, James Ethan Brent, Elizabeth Szekely, Karan Sheets as Editor and Designer, with special thanks to Bill Kluge for his help scanning many of the photographs and his contribution to the artwork for the cover.

We hope that proceeds from our joint efforts may contribute to the Gladys Davis Endowment Fund to extend the reach she promoted toward World Enlightenment. Thank You for sharing!

CONTENTS

PART ONE

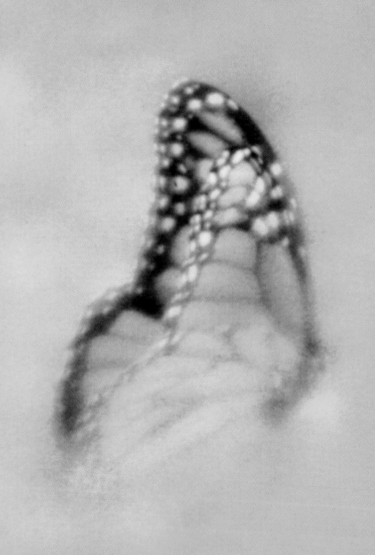

Angelic Introduction

As the heralds of springtime in the South spread the beauty of its floral greetings of 1904, a special Messenger appeared in the dream of Annie Wallace Davis, the young bride of Thomas Jefferson Davis. "You have been chosen to be the mother of a daughter whose name is Gladness!" Delighted to learn so early in her pregnancy the gender of the child she nurtured so happily, Annie felt the name so apropos as expressing the joy that Tom shared with her as eager parents.

The generations of today may be unaware that the more advanced technologies of twentieth century obstetrics were not yet available during the early decades. Such an announcement previewing a birth was exhilarating news. In her ecstasy of anticipation she awakened her husband to share the forecast. Sleepily he embraced her with enthusiasm matching her own as they shared their mutual blessing. Gregarious by nature, Tom found it impossible to withhold such news from his large extended family with whom they shared shelter.

The months ahead brought taunting reactions, teasing Annie that in her state of angelic awe she had misunderstood the name. "Surely, the name must have been Gladys, not Gladness," they chided her naiveté. Her own spirit of Gladness was rewarded with stamina and good health. Being of a cooperative nature as a dutiful wife of her culture's constrictions, Annie appeased tradition by allowing her daughter's birth certificate to list her as: Dorothy Gladys Davis, born January 30, 1905, Centerville, Alabama, USA, (thereby denying the use of her angelic title on it).

In the wee hours of that January morning, Annie and Thomas Jefferson Davis welcomed their promised daughter as the first of five healthy children. A rose is a rose. Gladys is Gladness, exhibiting the fulfilling joy as only she was intended to portray, just as her Angelic forecaster had so correctly prophesied. Gladness arrived as a gift to the Earth in a healthy physical body exactly as the herald angel had proclaimed to her mother; although given the name Gladys Davis, it was eventually to be paired with the spiritual mission of her twin soul, Edgar Cayce.

Edgar Cayce had been born on Sunday, March 18, 1877, to Carrie and Leslie Cayce of Christian County, Kentucky, with that same sense of purpose.

A Southern Star Appears

January 30, 1905, Centerville, Alabama, was a land of majestic magnolias, delta farms, country music and Southern Comfort. Vegetable gardens, fruits and nuts grew in profusion with cotton as King of the crops, as the South struggled to reconstruct its economy four decades past the devastating losses of the "War Between the States," as it was referred to in the land below the Mason-Dixon line. The dreaded boll weevil had not yet afflicted the cotton crops, but the challenges of financial woes still gripped the farm families who had lost their claims on large plantations. Most families shared the struggle to exist, while trying to save enough to buy a farm of their own, by being sharecroppers. Others gave up depending on the fates of weather and other factors that determined the crops production. If their skills or educational benefits allowed other options for employment, they often found it more profitable to move their families to towns, or cities, to survive or advance.

Whether it is called "The War Between The States," "The American Civil War," or any number of names, the tragic repercussions took their toll on the young nation. Physically and emotionally wounded, scars still blemish its history as a reminder of the experience.

It is difficult for later generations to comprehend all the motivations of either side of the conflict or evaluate the passions from a later state of cultural heritage. The many complications of individual emotions that fed their survival instincts are intricacies of misunderstanding. Whether its cause stemmed from the nation's history of struggle with slavery issues of North and South or unresolved political power strains in unfair economic controls, neither was fully resolved by its loss of thousands of lives and crippling injuries. Those years of warfare devastated the South.

Reconstruction after such drastic destruction was an overwhelming struggle after the horrors of that war, requiring more than a century for recuperation. Decades passed in restoration of farmlands that had lain fallow during much of the time their owners had exchanged plows for armor. Defeated soldiers returning to destitute families, unable to afford seed for planting the next years crop, presented a common plight. Deteriorated physical health, lack of emotional stamina and depressed attitudes factored with poverty as major challenges.

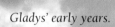

Gladys' early years.

Rural residents shared their strong sense of community by neighbors aiding neighbors. Every conceivable occasion that offered a way of celebrating their mutual cooperation nourished their spiritual revival. They had barn raisings, corn huskings, quilting parties and celebrated the harvesting of all crops. In the winter, putting up the hay and grains in the silos and barns, hog killing, curing their meats in smokehouses and chores of the season brought families together for work and play. Food and conversation was accompanied by music and dancing. Laughter and social interplay allowed their children to know and choose partners from established friendships.

Gladys' father was just such a good-natured neighbor, multi-talented, effervescent, a congenial young man, proudly carrying the label, Thomas Jefferson Davis, which summarized a family's gratitude for the distinction of both men (Thomas Jefferson and Jefferson Davis). Tom's love of music as a fiddler and singer made him a welcome participant at all the social events where young folks danced to celebrate their joint harvest chores. Gladys treasured him as a natural-born goodwill ambassador.

Church Revivals or community dances assured young couples of social connection and commitment invested toward providing healthy local governance and schools. Among Gladys' fondest memories of her father was the fun her "Papa" promoted in herding her mother, herself, two brothers and two younger sisters off to the Saturday night special event. Jovial greetings welcomed their appearance and followed their exits when they left to get their shut-eye, before rejoining most of the revelers at church services Sunday morning. Her mom was duly appreciated, too, as a hard-working farmer's partner when our conversations reverted to sharing our similar childhood memories. To be quite honest, though, both of us saw our fathers as the Joy-givers and our moms as the Job-givers.

Both Thomas Jefferson Davis and Annie Wallace Davis included their children in all ventures of neighborhood activities. Their bonds of love and joy sustained them through the years of shifting home sites wherever they could find an opportunity to farm. Starting their family in Centerville, the radius of their range expanded and fluctuated as financial situations affected their employers, or the labor markets offered Tom better advancements when children required larger shelters. Eventually, they settled in Selma, where their five children attended school and became actively engaged in local protestant churches.

In that era of rural America, each small town held its own distinctive flavor influenced by its founding families. Depending on the commerce that sustained each community's survival, its social structure flourished by necessity. Farmers diversified their crops and animal husbandry to provide their family sustenance through the year as independently as possible. Because their seasonal survival spanned so many variations from planting to reaping their harvest, each knew the value of family and friends' assistance, sharing each other's aid to bridge the gaps that nature provided consistently. Generations melded their varied talents to assure mutual survival to balance their social and psychological needs in education, healthcare and spiritual support. Businesses that thrived supplied the services needed to equip their economic expansion and exchange markets.

Such a magnet of multiple necessities centralized each region with congregational capsules forming townships which interspersed each area as our country's population multiplied. The early twentieth century America, using its iconic symbol, was like the young eaglet, developing its pin-feathers, barely flapping its downy wings in preparation for the soaring flights of the oversight of today's eclectic terrain. Its Southern habitat, devastated by the fires of war, was still a formidable nest of challenging opportunity from which to launch its flight into the future.

Choosing a course to pursue one's dream was daunting for those whose financial heritage was barren of an optimal green bank account. Fertile in faith, with humility and gratitude for simple rewards, each initial flight from its parents' nest lacked the gamble of falling from a high perch. The exhilaration may have been absent in the options of contemplation, but resignation to hold a dream sustained many serious teenagers. Stronger still, the pull, or push, that nags an inner urge to find expression drives determination to find a path that ventures from the mass pursuits of fellow travelers.

Gladys set her own course in seeking to appease such an urge, veering off the main track of student options to sharpen the tools that would be most applicable for her appointed rounds. Remote, at the time, it was there in a small town of only twenty-thousand people where Gladys met her destined

Gladys and her cousin, Mildred Davis.
Photo courtesy of the Edgar Cayce Foundation.

mission and, from her encounter with Edgar Cayce, the legacy of their joint accomplishments have circumnavigated our planet.

Born as the wave of "New Age" emphasis on religions with expansion of philosophical concerns of Life and Death opened new vistas of consideration, Gladys arrived from the Center of Being itself as a steward for Light. Humanity was being touched by a new awareness of purpose and goals of performance in a cyclic wave of spiritual search that affects areas, regions or countries like a fog lifting from the lowland marshes.

During the latter years of the preceding century, individuals of exceptionally persuasive drive were being born into different areas of America as the capacity for communication increased through radio waves, newspapers and postal service. Great orators and preachers evangelized their messages through travels to cultural centers of the country. Mary Baker Eddy's "Christian Science" spread her gospel through Reading Rooms. The Unity Village Mission, Theosophy groups and various fundamentalists set up tent meetings. Friends of the Quakers, Mormons and Brethren blanketed urban and rural areas where orthodox Christian Protestants, Catholic Churches, Jewish Synagogues and Temples were interspersed. Edgar Cayce, born in 1877, and Gladys Davis, born in 1905, came during the hey-day of the surge of renewed interests in spiritual and mystical devotion. Their contributions would become critical to the development of our spiritual responsibilities to this planet and to the Universe as a whole.

Leaving Selma High to attend a business school, Gladys soon acquired a job as a stenographer which allowed her to supplement her father's income for the family of seven. She was the first of their five children, with two younger brothers (Burt and Boyd) and two sisters (Mary Frances, or "Tiny," and Lucille). Cherished by loving parents and their extended families during the initial decades of the twentieth century, their family bonds were well-secured in mutual appreciation.

Thomas Jefferson Davis and his wife, Annie Wallace Davis, as sharecropping farmers, had moved around a lot as their young family grew, but they always kept strong family ties and good community relationships wherever they resided. Sharing of such responsibilities was an innate inheritance which Gladys found useful in her love of people and her work ethic throughout her life. Her talents and unique qualities of insight were soon to be assigned to a career which had no precedent in our modern world.

"Mister Cayce," as Gladys always respectfully called him, decided to hire a full-time secretary to record the "Readings," the term used for the psychic consultations he gave for clients seeking his intercession for spiritual aid. Gladys joined a fellow employee of Tissier's Hardware Store to record her first event of attending one of Edgar Cayce's psychic Readings. Being unaware of the job opening until after Miss Willie Graham, manager of Tissier's china department, had delivered Gladys' typed copy to Mr. Cayce, Gladys was surprised when told, "He was impressed with your accuracy and wants to talk with you if you are interested in the job."

Having discussed the strange episode of witnessing and recording Mr. Cayce's "clairvoyant" reading with her friend Ruth, who had helped her decipher some of its anatomical terminology, Gladys shared with her the news of his job offer. Ruth was ecstatic, since she was intrigued with stories of his record of the miraculous recoveries of those who had followed the instructions as they were given. Gladys talked with her mother about it, too, and the next day she eagerly made her way up the steps to his studio.

As a result of her attunement and accuracy, Mr. Cayce hired her as his permanent secretary. She was happy to be hired for the opportunity of her lifetime! As time often proves, Fate is not accidental. Edgar Cayce recognized those whom God had sent to serve, even while he was awake.

At the time of his hiring Gladys no relocation appeared imminent, but the opportunities that led to his departure from Selma were backstage, in the wings of development. So, Gladys climbed the steps to their home adjoining his photography studio to be introduced to Gertrude and her small son, Edgar Evans, on her first day of her new employment. Their initial contact was congenially comfortable as Mrs. Cayce welcomed her with an assortment of his past records, an accumulated puzzle of irregular papers, as notes from previous Readings.

Mrs. Cayce explained the "menagerie collection" as notes taken by various witnesses during Readings that her husband had given during the preceding years. Requests for his unusual assistance to the sick and injured seemed to be spreading through stories of the patients' improvements, and had increased enough that Mr. Cayce felt the dire need of a stenographer. From the presentation of cluttered scraps, an obvious employment decision was verified. Gladys accepted the challenge with gratitude for having studied shorthand, typing, filing and organizing records which prepared her with skills for this unique opportunity. She rolled up her sleeves.

To familiarize her with the language and procedures used in acquiring the information sought in each case, Gladys was introduced to the eclectic collection of sketchy scraps of words. Some few had been typed, others handwritten, legible or vaguely decipherable, while others were summarized versions as after-thoughts of directions given.

Mrs. Cayce patiently explained the variety of experiences and people involved in their acquisitions and dispensations, summing up her husband's desire for greater efficiency needed to assure that correct application be asserted for their use. Gladys sensed Gertrude's reluctance to push or to pull back Edgar's services, since she owed her own survival from tuberculosis to the help given through his "Readings."

While Mr. Cayce was called away to aid an old friend in Ohio, the two continued their preparatory orientation for Gladys' secretarial services. Upon his return, Mr. Cayce was revved up with inspiration of having opened a new avenue of informational research use for study. Arthur Lammers and Linden Shroyer had added astrological influences to the search and reincarnation implications were introduced. Arthur Lammers offered a proposition to employ him as a full time psychic if he would move his family to Ohio. Gertrude was persuaded to move, and so was Gladys, trusting the change as freedom for expanded opportunity.

Edgar Cayce was on the verge of alterations in adapting his unusual array of talents at the time of hiring a stenographer. Circumstances stirred up movements in his life that moved his employment from Selma, Alabama, to Dayton, Ohio, and his skills as an artistic photographer to the full-time use of his innate insights in the realm of psychic phenomena. Strange as Edgar Cayce may have seemed to those who had heard of his unusual diagnostic skills, the breadth of his clairvoyant range had no known parallel in 1923 when he chose Gladys for the job of recording his psychic consultations. Stranger still were the revelations yet to be expressed.

On the threshold of adulthood, Gladys was being re-introduced to knowledge of astrological influences, past incarnations and previews of future events as dream interpretations unraveled their mysteries. Edgar Cayce was simultaneously being re-wired for their assignment, along with his family members and friends, too, who had been drawn into the vortex of their purpose for incarnating at this time. Leaving her family home to accept the challenge of this commitment, her life was destined to be forever after uniquely different in every aspect from all others.

Leaving the nuts and bolts accounting of Tissier's Hardware Store in Selma, Alabama, to record the messages of a universe that soared over the rainbows of her dreams, she was freed from the mundane gravity of her rural and small town tethers. New vistas opened as Gladys joined Mr. Cayce's family in their new Ohio environs. His self-induced trances, from which he expressed answers to questions posed in behalf of the clients seeking aids in their challenging predicaments, faced diversions that altered the course of all involved thereafter. Revelations cast light on subjects beyond the scope of his previous scrutiny and understanding.

Leaving their elder son, Hugh Lynn, in Selma with friends to graduate with his senior classmates of high school, the family ventured together toward their new horizons. Joining the family household of Edgar and Gertrude, Gladys bonded with a wholesome familiarity in their relationships with each other. Each grew in understanding of their interwoven spiritual cords as the years progressed. Along with their series of past ventures as channels of God's healing influences to uplift all of His individual cells, or souls, came a renewal of their contract to serve once more as His Ambassadors. As they shared the challenges of each day, these increments of revelation unfolded gradually as they studied explanations given in their dreams, meditations and the Readings.

Moving on to Ohio, Edgar Cayce realized that his paramount soul mission was to commit to the Work of giving Readings for the benefit of others as his full-time career. Edgar, Gertrude and Gladys, united again in this life, faced a refresher course in memory. Through their expanded contacts, a broader scope of subjects shook their cultural and religious beliefs from the moorings of conventional awareness. Met at first with cautionary resistance as they struggled to align the vast scope of the Readings with the more constrained doctrines of their culture, their discussions were inspired by their strong ties of religious adherence. Instead of creating divisions, many concepts from the Readings bridged gaps towards a greater cohesion of their beliefs. Never was there a call to abandon their institutions of faith; instead, they were inspired to strengthen their bonds with tolerant views from other angles.

Life Readings gave insights of relationships during previous lifetimes, where each individual was encouraged to pursue with dedication the guidance of one's intuition in serving God's Will, as attunement with the Source supplants any human desires which may have detrimental consequences to the soul's progress in life. Hardships as stumbling blocks became the stepping stones to higher vistas of understanding as a course in spiritual development.

When the Readings introduced the links with former lifetimes, their religious beliefs were sorely tested. Each participant was stimulated by personal choices and adjustments. They struggled with the concept and their reliance on the spiritual source of information as being God-inspired, concluding eventually that Truth reigned Faith. Communication bridges with old friends and family concepts kept Gladys suspended in a defensive atmosphere, as her loved ones anxiously envisioned a demonic threat destroying her religious route to Heaven, while she managed to sustain her ground against the tide of the prejudice of their limited understanding. The whole Cayce family had their similar concerns and kept a prayerful vigilance about the new revelations.

Reincarnation was a foreign theory to the Western Theological mind and America's Bible-based Religions. These new concepts, while intriguing to many, were viewed as barriers by those who feared reincarnation as a fundamental threat to their belief system.

This photo, taken by Edgar Cayce, of his wife, Gertrude, and Gladys with young Edgar Evans in Dayton, OH, in 1924. Photo courtesy of the Edgar Cayce Foundation.

His Shift in Consciousness

When Edgar Cayce applied himself to channel the message of a Reading, a basic ritual was utilized. Removing his shoes, loosening his tie, or belt, he lay on his back upon a couch, relaxing a moment in prayer or meditation. Sitting beside him, a conductor would wait until the flutter of his eyelids signaled readiness to take questions. While in an altered state of consciousness via auto-hypnosis, he was given suggestions by the conductor followed by the questions in behalf of the client. As scribe, Gladys recorded in shorthand

the questions and answers as voiced. A copy would be typed for the inquirer with a carbon copy for the physician and one to be retained in Mr. Cayce's file.

The information gleaned from each session was recorded by Gladys as a "Reading." Thousands of them, archived by coded numbers, have proven to be uncannily accurate. Through the years, various individuals acted as conductors and scribes, not always bringing satisfactory results. Even Mr. Lammers' setup was not always ideal when they first collaborated. Ultimately, it was Gertrude who served best in the conductor's role.

Since the information exceeded his conscious knowledge, Mr. Cayce credited the Readings to the Source of Life, or God. Spiritually oriented throughout his life, he had devoted much time to Bible study and his desire to serve as his intuition directed.

Although he had performed in giving Readings for various entities who sought his services, Arthur Lammers' interests in astrology brought the theory of reincarnation into play, so that each member of the Cayce family was given "Life Readings," as they came to be listed. Past lives were mentioned not just in physical health studies, although the first reference to a physical ailment which originated in a previous period of history was the trigger which opened the floodgate's deluge of curiosity.

Astrology and reincarnation added the elements of mystical health issues, having their roots in past experiences that plagued individuals from soul memories. The law of Karma, or cause and effect, from past lives awakened controversial religious beliefs for our Western civilization with a force that had been basically ignored for centuries.

The Readings gave explanations that proved helpful when Edgar Cayce's health was impaired, as well as for the clients who sought cures and guidance. Readings made references to periods of history of which none of the listeners had ever imagined, such as Egypt, and before that, back to Atlantis, even before Adam, as we identify Earth's first human.

The phenomena of miraculous cures from his previous "Physical Readings" had stirred the interest of a skeptical news fringe that was gaining in popularity and increased his clientele for awhile. Then, their flow trickled to almost a standstill, and Mr. Lammers' financial backing dried up. Edgar Cayce's economic status had never been worse.

In Dayton, Ohio, David Kahn, a longtime friend and an avid advocate, introduced Edgar Cayce to his friend, Morton Blumenthal, a young, outstanding Wall Street financier. Morton sought interpretations of his dreams, another realm of new inquiry. As his involvement progressed, Morton's depth of scholarship of the Kabala proved to make him one of the most interesting individuals to join the ranks. His inquiries brought forth answers that are sought by all who seek to understand their relationship with God as our Life Force. Coupled with Tom Sugrue's Life Readings and many later enlistees whose Life Readings brought floods of such pertinent data to the archived cache of Cayce's work, we are enriched by their contributions. It was primarily by Morton's family and their associates that Virginia Beach became the world headquarters of Edgar Cayce's Library. Instigating the construction of the Cayce Hospital and the Cavalier Hotel, the first luxury class tourist attraction on its sands, they seeded the pearl that initiated its expansion to become Virginia's largest city.

When Arthur Lammers' business failed, the family faced a period of financial challenge worse than any Gladys could ever remember. Yet, Providence interceded to reassure that, at the most dire moments, they need never fear lack of provisions. Contacts with those whose participation forged groundwork for future expansion of the Work, especially by the Blumenthal brothers, led to their move in establishing a central headquarters at Virginia Beach, Virginia.

This twist of fate, however, brought native caution to new dimensions of religious defenses, placing their survival situation in dire jeopardy. Serious consideration and prayerful analysis were applied while bravely trusting the Source of all Supply. The family persevered as new recruits, such as Thomas B. Brown, Morton and his brother, Edwin Blumenthal, and others, appeared on the scene. Their passion for the seer's talents outdistanced all previous clients as they rescued the Cayce family from poverty. Eager to have access for their interests, they arranged to have the family move East. Mr. Cayce, guided by intuition, meditation, Readings, Gertrude and family conferences, settled on a site of spiritual guidance and their mutual agreement to fulfill the plan as God directed. So, the Cayce's move to Virginia where the Cayce Hospital was built was financed, fulfilling a life-long dream of Edgar Cayce toward healing the sick.

Astronomical Assignment

Edgar Cayce's translations of the Akashic Records did for souls in search of spiritual truths what the Hubble Space Telescope does for stargazers and astronomers. Whereas the Hubble reveals clearer images of distant celestial objects than ever seen before, the Akashic Records enlighten seekers with the clarity and scope of their revelations. They are astounding to those who have found access to their contents. Gladys archived each snapshot of Edgar Cayce's experience as vividly as Hubble's celestial transmissions, magnifying his accomplishments as a transmitter of spiritual inspiration.

In re-establishing a school of inspiration for entities seeking further enlightenment, Edgar Cayce and Gladys' efforts magnetized the spirit of cooperation which soon drew global support of kindred souls whose mission was to share the "Work" load. From their arrival in Virginia in September, 1925, their mission attracted workers who had previously contributed their services toward its fulfillment. Former participants continued to support the cause from Kentucky, Alabama, Ohio, New York and elsewhere. Concepts for an educational ministry and the expansion of healing arts services thrived with their financial and spiritual support. Meager sustenance afforded housing, food and clothing for the Cayce household, while confirming their faith and inspiration to pursue expansion of their dreams.

As the local residents gradually adapted cautious acceptance of their benefits, the Cayce Hospital was built under the auspices of a Board of Trustees, funded mainly by the Blumenthal brothers, their friends and associates of New York. While living in Dayton, relationships with Morton and Edwin had blossomed. Moving to Virginia was due to pragmatic convenience and the Universal guidance of Cayce's Readings which established the ideal location of their joint healing mission.

Community disciples expanded goodwill as they observed patients receiving "strange treatments." A few brave souls formed special groups for prayer, healing and Bible study under Mr. Cayce's tutelage. Branches of those Study Groups formed in New York and elsewhere as news circulated about the phenomenal benefits received by their participants.

Magazine articles and other news releases brought attention and growth to the membership advocates as Atlantic University was planned for the site.

The "Roaring Twenties" was heralding a new age of development in the South as the Cavalier Hotel was raised to house the North's tourists. Among them were many attracted to the "Miracle Man of Virginia," as Edgar Cayce was becoming known.

Against the backdrop of this period of rapid development, the trumpet sounded as the modern-day prophet brought forth his forecast of changes in the world's future, while his faithful scribe determined that the Readings must survive for the generations that follow.

Gladys and her cousin, Mildred Davis.
Photo courtesy of the Edgar Cayce Foundation.

It was not long, however, before personal differences in priority on the focus of Edgar Cayce's attention began to erode trust between the philanthropists and the Hospital Board. Jealousies between individuals in controlling their financial roles ensued. Ignoring the advice of the Readings, a wrong turn was made. Misunderstandings increased, as the economic woes of Wall Street in 1929 brought havoc affecting the financial supporters, disrupting productive relationships between institutional managers and eventually leading to the closing of the Cayce Hospital. Emotions, egos and economics created weapons of divisive strain. Injuries scarred their former attunement and orchestrated a crescendo of cymbals as that era of cooperative partnership crashed to its finale.

Devastated by the loss of his personal dream, the Cayce Hospital, intended to help heal the sick and disabled who sought his aid, Edgar Cayce showed signs of depression as never before. Although the prognosis of her continued employment must have presented its bleak finality, Gladys focused her attention on the needs of others. Her "Considerosity" was applied to the disheartened warriors as she sought to cheer them past the crisis, in spite of the bridges collapsing beyond repair around her.

At such times of challenge, Gladys' true nature beamed. Stamina, practicality and innate persistence kept her pushing forward. Applying faith, as the Readings had admonished them to do, she rallied the remnant survivors to gain strength through the shield of prayer and meditation of forgiveness. Mr. Cayce's Readings, she just knew, would direct them through the valley, dispel the shadow of defeat and open the barriers for crossing to the Promised Land. Surely, God would show another option for Mr. Cayce's remarkable gifts.

With the closing of the hospital, no one was more acutely affected by the gloom of despair than Cayce himself. Gladys and his immediate family members were keenly aware of the need for his sense of purpose being sustained for the sake of all who had depended on his leadership. Her role as his devoted secretary faced its peril if courage failed to promote necessary change, so she dared to instigate her own intuitive plan. Writing letters and pleas for feedback from former beneficiaries of his services became her tools to gain inertia. It worked. Responses of "Gladitude" from the beneficiaries of the Readings' inspiration began to flow.

Gladys, after contacting the local leaders of their Bible study and prayer groups to alert them of Mr. Cayce's apparent dejection and seek more support in his behalf, dared to expand her plea to a few others. Since so many contacts in New York, particularly, were bridged through the Kahns, she wrote an emotionally charged note to David, explaining the destitution that the family faced as they faced losing their rented home. He, in turn, contacted others of mutual interests. When some financial concerns were shown by those who responded, she was apologetic that she had acted via emotional anxiety rather than by her normal trust in the Lord's Providence. Faith is great, but as channels of God's supply route, we have to act on our intuition, even daring to cross lines of new territory. Her youth and role in the scheme of "employment," probably led her to feel inadequate, but her passion was valid about the situation jeopardizing the Work and Mr. Cayce's role in it. Passive, she was not, thank heavens.

Benevolence was expressed through the gratitude of those who had realized the benefits of Mr. Cayce's Readings in healing their afflictions of mind, body and soul. The pace of donations increased, helping to sustain the family. Centers were established in urban and rural areas, as two volumes of *"Search For God"* books and many articles, magazines and books were published about the organization's focus. "Cooperation" as the first lesson was exemplified as the remnants of the hospital staff and local participants were quilted together in a coalition of renewed support.

The Cayce Hospital had drawn an influx of dedicated staffers to move their families to the sparsely inhabited beach resort. The staff and new organization members, with local prayer and meditation groups, formed a charter called the Association for Research and Enlightenment. Individual Readings were still available as were those for groups. Guidance Readings for Board of Directors, annual Congress events, Bible Study, prayer and healing groups, coordinated the Work locally and in the expanding fields of endeavor throughout the land. The first Association of National Investigators had been legally dissolved at Morton Blumenthal's office in New York, ending their relationship while closing all ties with the hospital.

So, 1931 began a new phase of application for Edgar Cayce's expertise that kept his family at the beach. Buying their first home with the help of family

Gladys, Edgar Cayce, his wife, Gertrude, and Gladys' nephew, T.J., in the Cayce Garden.
Photo courtesy of the Edgar Cayce Foundation.

and friends was a healing tonic for a new outlook on life. Many changes in their lives brought stability. As a homeowner at last, Edgar Cayce could enjoy communion with nature and exercise in the open, sea-washed air. He found adding to their bounty by gardening and fishing as soul-refreshing and among his favorite pursuits.

For the first time in his life, he reaped the benefit of owning property, a home and garden that meant Cayce could settle into planting crops that he could harvest. Stability is rewarding and inspirational. At last, a head-quarters could be established for the magnetism of seekers of Truth. Gladys' future employment was assured in the role for which she was uniquely prepared with her Sunny disposition for spreading its warmth and healing rays on all whose lives she touched. Through the ensuing years, she continued in the role of Cayce's efficient scribe and Gertrude's devoted friend and home assistant. Their generous sharing of hearth and hearts endowed her sense of harmony and security. No other job in the world was more appealing to her.

It's amazing that, out of such a period of doubt and lack of resources, the impetus for the *"Search for God"* books came. It is a point which bears amplification. While Cayce was defeated, depressed and grieving, Gladys was rising on the upswing, rallying the troops, inspiring those around them to action. The synergy which the family exercised is laudable; when one was down, the other picked up the cross. Grace, faith and contagion of a motivated "Gladness" pulled them through the difficulties while directly inspiring the essential path outlined by the *"Search for God"* books, a master key to the Work.

"When one door closes, another opens." Life proves its theory as in their case, when "keeping on" meant a re-focus on priorities. Emphasized was the dedication of participants in the Search for God groups in applying efforts to study Universal Laws, as Edgar Cayce's Readings focused humbled hearts and minds in a receptive stance for guidance. Seeking mercy and grace as a necessity of survival is a powerful motivator of attentive listening. The lessons of this period were forever etched in their minds as they moved forward with renewed purpose.

The economic "Depression" crashed hopes with its big stick, affecting changes around the world. Edgar Cayce's Readings helped to bring Spiritual Authority back in vogue for an enlarged audience. Reaching outward to the community, his family and friends spread the Word, applying the advice of the Readings through deeds to prove their merit, while Edgar Cayce discovered a renewed sense of purpose teaching his Sunday School class and focussing on the Readings.

The Cayce Home on Arctic Circle, Virginia Beach, Virginia

Expanding Options

When Gladys' infant nephew became her temporary ward in 1936, Gertrude and Edgar welcomed the expansion of family by sharing every aspect of his care with Gladys. The harmony of their home on Arctic Circle reflected the warmth of their previous lifetimes as a family in Persia, with slight alterations in casting. Where in that Persian period, Edgar (as Uhjltd) was married to Gladys (Ilya), and Gertrude (Inxa) was his niece who was adopted by the couple, in this century, the roles were flipped. Unity of spirit merged their blended family roles in work and play much akin to the cooperation their lives had manifested in their past associations.

Gladys' family had always linked her heart with loving concerns, and she drew her siblings toward Virginia as they matured. Her brother, Boyd, and his wife, Burlyn, lived nearby when their only son was born. As an alcoholic, Burlyn's breast-milk was poisonous to her baby, whose fragile health stressed her tenuous balance as a new mother. Gladys was their anchor of hope as she assumed the task of her nephew's care. She enlisted Mr. Cayce's diagnosis to save the child's life. Recognizing the infant soul at first sight, Edgar Cayce welcomed him with life-preserving aid.

There are no accidents in God's plan of reincarnation for His Workers, as their lives exemplified. Love, like rich cream, rises to top off the flow of milk and honey in all of our relationships with one another. It retains its respect and recognition of our ongoing soul development, no matter how the circumstances may alter the physical roles we draw. By the same law, as one of Gladys' own Readings informed her in answer to her question about a sibling, the qualities of their former relationship would continue the challenges they faced before until soul changes were accomplished. Just as harmony or discord in compatibility are comparable to mixing oil and water, the elements matter in attitudes as well.

Although her Life Reading stated that through her family she would experience rewarding satisfaction, she did not choose to marry until past forty years of age, after Edgar and Gertrude Cayce had passed on. Even then, her work with the Cayce Foundation (and its progeny, A.R.E.) was paramount.

She welcomed the parental care role of her infant nephew, while living in the Cayce home, where Gertrude and Edgar had joined in saving his fragile life. As the infant was brought inside, Edgar Cayce greeted him immediately

Gladys holding her nephew, Thomas Jefferson Davis.
On the following pages, Edgar Cayce and T.J. fishing.
B&W photos courtesy of the Edgar Cayce Foundation.
Mr. Cayce's hat, which T.J. has kept to this day, is shown as an inset.

as Thomas Jefferson, verified by a Reading shortly thereafter. Gladys' father was also named Thomas Jefferson Davis, while Edgar Cayce's grandfather, was named Thomas Jefferson Cayce. "Now here is Thomas Jefferson himself, back in America!" Edgar Cayce announced to the anxious group.

Now, "T.J." (#1208), as most of us came to know him, was truly the reincarnated author of The Declaration of Independence, back again in our midst. His presence in their household was bonded with appreciation that long ago was linked by strong karmic ties to each of them. A series of Readings given for various early American pioneers fill in details of that incarnation. His life as Alexander the Great, as his Reading describes, and previous relationships with Edgar Cayce and his Aunt Gladys are an interesting study of their soul connections and provide lesser known historical details. His Readings offer revelations of benefit to any serious student of history when paired with Mr. Cayce's repertoire of insights and the characters whose lives were revealed through his unique psychic lens.

In 1936, as Adolf Hitler was rising to power in Europe, the soul of Thomas Jefferson was being reincarnated in Virginia Beach, Virginia. I don't pretend to understand the cycle of souls, or how God plans their schedules, but I do find such contrasting shifts in focus interesting as history unfurls its opportunities. Was America being reminded of its role in denouncing tyrannical rule as evil threatened the freedoms endorsed by its founders?

Edgar Cayce's Readings revealed the connections to a number of former patriots of the Early American era during that decade Of interest to me, also, is that Thomas Jefferson, as a Deist, would be drawn to Cayce, a confirmed Christian, who gave Readings promoting the unity of worshippers of all faiths to be attentive to One Source of All Supply.

Their bonding had been divinely ordained, according to Readings of that pre-Atlantean timespan which predates Adam. As peers of Amilius, the first expression of the Divine Mind of Christ who led souls into the earth plane in spirit form, Edgar and Gladys acted as Guardians for T.J. during that lifetime, leading him to work for the Sons of Light. More details can be found in many Readings, especially in the Atlantis Series.

"Tommy," as they called him then, as an addition to their household, brought a new dimension to each of their lives. Being critically ill on arrival, Mr. Cayce's Reading for him brought concise directions for his formula needs and overall care, saving the infant's tenuous hold on life. Gladys, then at 31, welcomed her brother's firstborn as a soul that she had long held dear, having been his special guardian since pre-Atlantean associations. With both sons now grown, though still single, Mr. and Mrs. Cayce were very gracious in adding the infant to their extended family. Devotion to care of the child seemed to enhance "Gladness" with each sign of its success. Tommy's survival and signs of development rewarded all concerned, although interaction with his alcoholic parents remained chaotic throughout his childhood.

Tommy's bassinet was always within reach as Gladys took dictation, typed, or filed the transcripts and correspondence that grew more abundant as time progressed. Like attentive grandparents, both Edgar and Gertrude shared in his loving care and bonding. Since their home was headquarters for all the Work, people were in and out constantly every day as their duties increased with growing membership. Yet somehow, Mr. Cayce managed to keep gardening and fishing, finding ways to incorporate Tommy's outings in the

fresh air and sunshine as he did so. At the same time, the schedule for Readings grew longer as well.

As a toddler out of the crib, the family faced some challenging moments in Tommy's development. Incidents as the one described earlier, where the lone child wandered outside, heading toward Lake Holly when Mr. Cayce's awareness of danger alerted him during his "unconscious Reading-state." That, for me, is intriguing to ponder. Was his connection to Tommy's welfare, or to other loved ones near him, so prevalent that his consciousness veered from the role of his "mental trance state"? Was the capacity of oneness of the various levels of mind in sync always? Was the spiritual link of his twin soul so vital that her distraction of viewing the child's danger created a short circuit, altering his mental attunement to the Reading? The mind is such a mysterious aspect of our nature. Edgar Cayce's adept use of the mind's myriad facets offers us a tantalizing opportunity for study.

Fishing as he sat on the pier, or on the float that he had adorned with the potted willow tree for shade, Mr. Cayce often was accompanied by Tommy, whom he treated as an associate as he talked aloud about his concerns. While keeping the child entertained, the exercise of expressing matters which he normally shared in lectures or Sunday School Bible classes was good practice in coordinating his subject matter. Like a mental sponge, T.J. was soaking up the essence of Life's purpose as few children have the opportunity to experience lessons. The scarcity of playmates in the neighborhood, meant that adults exclusively were his constant companions. Meeting spiritual scholars, Eastern mystics and dignitaries from other cultures who sought Cayce's counsel on spiritual matters or world events were common occurrences in their household. Not since his life as Alexander had T.J. experienced such audiences, and so fitting that Alexander would sit at the feet of Edgar and provide the sounding board for Cayce's thoughts.

T.J. shared one of his childhood memories where Mr. Cayce showed a daily interest in the development of one of his favorite plants, a small apple tree. When it finally produced its first fruit, there remained only one apple to reach maturity on it. Checking on its progress was a daily routine as he shared the rounds with Tommy. At last he beamed with special pride as they viewed its perfection. Allowing the child to play in the yard, he gathered his fishing gear. "Today I want to taste that specimen with my fish fry *du jour*," clicking his tongue, he announced to Tommy with a knowing wink. The little boy responded with the wink that he had recently learned to mimic.

So while the fish were studying Edgar's baited hook, T.J. concentrated on the tempting apple. When he could no longer fight the impatient urge, he tested his reach. Holding the specimen apple in both his hands, nature's impulse applied its teeth to the surface of appeal. Enjoying its flavor with the relish of Thomas Jefferson tasting the contents of his famous wine cellar collection, his conscious awareness reeked with guilt. With one more bite, he sought a place to hide its remains.

Having prepared his catch for the frying pan, Edgar trekked toward the apple tree's prize reward. As the pain of disbelief gripped the entire stature of the man he lovingly called "Eddie Caykee," Tommy bowed his head in shame. "I ate it," he admitted.

"Where is the core?" Mr. Cayce asked, hoping at least to save the apple's seed. Tommy retrieved it from the tuft of its floral nest and handed it to the tall man he adored. With a pat on the child's sunny-red head, he took the ragged apple with his left hand, and the boy's hand in his right as they marched in the kitchen for their midday feast.

While still of pre-school age, T.J. received a bow and arrow as a gift, which he welcomed with joy. Since their neighbors found Mr. Cayce's psychic reputation disconcerting, their children often taunted the child when he played outside alone. One, the son of a policeman who was about ten years old, bullied Tommy by shooting at him with his BB gun as he played in the street that fronted their homes and had become a constant threat to keep the child away from his buddies. T.J. decided to fend off such abuse. Gathering a stash of cattails that grew on the banks of the lake, he dried them in the sun. Finally he saw his opportunity as the Bully played in the street.

Using one of Mr. Cayce's cigarette lighters, he lit a dry cattail, and using his brand new bow, sent it on its soaring flight toward the dreaded adversary. The burning torch zoomed upward in its glorious arc, far beyond his wildest dream, glowing brilliantly as it traveled across the street, uh oh..., descending on the roof of The Star of the Sea. Landing in a gutter full of autumn leaves, the fiery flames danced as they consumed the leaves, then the shingles and the rafters of the Catholic Church building. The whole structure was engulfed before the fire trucks could arrive. The building was wrapped in a flaming blanket, as sirens blared en route, and all the residents of the area witnessed the disaster.

Police cars, Fire Department vehicles, and masses of onlookers created chaos as seldom seen in the small town that served as a tourist Mecca by the sea. Young as he was, Tommy realized his blame in the disaster, as the dread of his fate dawned on his conscience. Anticipating the threatening condemnation of the Archangel Michael, whose booming voice he recalled hearing through one of Edgar Cayce's Readings, brought fear to surface in his trembling body. There was no escape from the unintended consequences of his effort to defend himself from his adversaries.

When he had told his Aunt Gladys about being shot at by the policeman's son, she had consoled him with the fact that God was protecting him. He was to thank God every day for His love and protection. Fear was a no-no. But, God was so busy, like her, and everybody, maybe even more so. He tried to keep her from sharing his doubts. Mr. Cayce didn't need them either. What's a fellow to do, when all his efforts backfire? This is one huge backfire. The Catholic Sanctuary turned into ashes by a flaming cattail shot from his bow. Self persecution whirled endlessly. As the vehicles departed and the crowd dispersed, Mr. Cayce coaxed him to go into their home. Penitently he followed, unsure of his defense plans, but God must have heard his pleas.

Father Brennan called out to them, "Wait, Mr. Cayce, I want to hug Tommy." His face glowed, not from the heat of the fire, but wreathed in a smile that seemed to surprise them both. As one of Edgar Cayce's closest friends of Virginia Beach, and Tommy's too, their greatest concern for the loss

The Star of the Sea Catholic Church

of his Church was for his pain. Yet, here he was, waiving a sheaf of papers in the air as he smiled upon them. "I have been praying for help to expand our Sanctuary and getting no encouragement from our congregation or the Diocese. When I found these papers on its insurance coverage, I have checked, and learned that we were over-insured to the degree that we can rebuild with the expansion we need. God can be counted on to multiply the benefits for Job's losses, if the Faith is in His Providence. Thank you, Tommy, for helping God to answer my prayers."

In 1936, as the world was afflicted with extreme chaos, clouds of war intensified. Urges for Cayce's prophetic insight also increased. When the Fates had moved her infant nephew into her lap, and Edgar and Gertrude had expanded their arms and generous hearts to add the child to their family space, Gladys was then given the maternal role of responsibility for his temporary care. Her duties associated with Mr. Cayce's Readings and his paternal guidance of the organization were not diminished as they all shared in restoration of the little boy's health and early education.

She coped with Tommy's parents in their constant disharmony, knowing what devastating effects such behavior has on the lives of their children, and the generations that follow. Such karmic connections are powerful elements of disturbing distractions, as a study of T.J.'s life indicates. When a soul with so much potential for service to the masses, even with the adoration of guardians like Mr. Cayce and Gladys, enters through unstable parents, the odds are stacked for spiritual warfare. The patience and fortitude of Gladys and Mr. Cayce's prayers and faith were tested daily.

The Readings refer to the former relationship of Gladys' guardianship of T.J. during his lifetime as Alexander the Great. It seems she helped him as an advisor as he conquered various lands, sometimes in charismatic alignments of personal magnetism, at others in mastery of physical force or cunning. The Readings forewarned that during this lifetime T.J. would face the ultimate challenge of conquering self under extenuating circumstances. Granted, Gladys' desire to help him was no less than what she had expended in the past, but only T.J. could make decisions involved in mastering self.

Entering as an unhealthy infant, fragile life survival struggles seemed to surround each phase of his childhood while the chaotic succession of tossed and turned events gave Gladys little control over his early training and educational adjustments. Distractions in moving him from pillar to posts, as his estranged parents vied for control over his life throughout their own instabilities, kept her constantly concerned. Yet in loving patience, she bravely persevered as the stable hitching post for family cohesiveness through traumas few others could have endured with such emotional balance.

Mr. and Mrs. Cayce were anchors of great strength for her, as they shared her anxieties for the special child whose life linked theirs in mutual adoration and concern. Having exhibited strong physical and intelligent mastery in past lifetimes, this soul chose the ideal environment of their support to face the challenges he entered this life to meet. Studying his life path presents one of the most mysterious karmic puzzles that I have ever encountered. Intriguing dichotomy exists to veil analysis justly by any outsider.

Continuing family support for her widowed mother and younger siblings, Gladys formed an axis of stability for their maturation. Gladys' family was always her precious concern and beneficiary. Her brothers and youngest sister were drawn to the area as they began families of their own. Her nephews and nieces shared the aura of her affection, as did my children and grandchildren. Hugh Lynn and Edgar Evans' families knew the marvel of her devotion as well.

Her own nesting instincts led to sharing space in a duplex home arrangement with her brother, as the Cayce home became so much more crowded as headquarters for the expanding Work. The staff had grown as demands for the membership services expanded through a broader public awareness of Mr. Cayce's remarkable expertise.

Gladys at her first home, Glad Niche, in 1950.
Photo courtesy of the Edgar Cayce Foundation.

Life at their overloaded facility, scheduled Readings, meetings, lectures and printed literature grew more hectic, especially as World War II captured the concern of the world.

During this period, Gladys re-encountered an old friend from the Persian era, Mrs. Louise Chisholm (#1152), whose Life Readings identified her as the Innkeeper's daughter of Bethlehem. She had held the newborn baby Jesus, which renewed the bond which lingered through the years from helping Gladys care for Him during His Persian incarnation as Zend. Their friendship shared a mutual link with Irene and Milton Harrison, who in that lifetime were Jesus' sister, Ruth (#1158), and Philoas (#1151), His Roman brother-in-law. In 1950, Mrs. Chisholm deeded the property to Gladys on which she built her own beloved "Glad Niche," where she lived the remainder of her life. At age 45, for the first time, Gladys had a home of her own. Such was the extent of her sacrifice to support her family and accomplish her life's mission with the Work.

Search For God Groups

When Edgar Cayce was reincarnated on March 18, 1877, to begin this phase of his God-given mission, the field of endeavors was being prepared for a new crop of concepts. Heretofore, the seeds planted in the Garden of Eden had suffered alterations which impaired them when falling on poor soil. Negligent, self-centered stewards, through eons of history, failed to cultivate conditions that preserved ideal attributes by allowing weeds of abuse to suffocate the growth of grains of Truth.

Norfolk Study Group Number One as photographed by Edgar Cayce in 1932.
Photo courtesy of the Edgar Cayce Foundation.

Misconceptions have altered the harvest of ideals throughout mankind's dominance of this physical plane, so that need for honest stewardship required a renewed perspective. The soul of Ra-Ta, Uhjltd, Lucius, or Edgar Cayce, as we know him today, was called again to enter the vineyard. Using the tools developed through his past incarnations, he practiced their application throughout his youth in preparation for the challenges of awakening all fellow souls to the task before us as God's children.

Out of adversity and times of testing, periods of great growth and expansion often arise. For Edgar Cayce, developing of the *"Search for God"* books and the Association of Research and Enlightenment marked the beginning of a period of intense development for all involved. The Introduction of the *"Search for God, Book One"* states:

> The eternal question that runs through life is this: What is truly valuable in thought, in activity and in experience? Only from within can come a stable estimate of what is worthwhile. This sense of appreciation or this inner realization is based fundamentally upon an understanding of self—self in relation to others and self in relation to God. Meditation is the means to this end. *(page 5, Search for God, Book One)*

The two small *"Search for God"* books came from Readings which outlined a series of affirmations and ideals for use by individuals and groups to increase spiritual awareness through meditation, prayer and discussion. The original Search for God groups attracted extraordinarily well-attuned, unique and inspiring individuals whose paths, they recognized, had crossed in lifetimes before. This group of dedicated individuals formed a foundation whose positive energies helped Edgar Cayce sustain his continued efforts to bring the Readings to searching souls, while inspiring him to stay attuned to his sense of purpose.

A composite of people appeared whose spiritual base linked their former lives with his, especially during Egyptian, Persian, Judean and Early American ventures of applied leadership and cooperation through the use of prayer and meditation. As interest in the *"Search for God"* books spread throughout America and eventually overseas, they have continued to guide all who choose to follow their map in self-preparation for greater understanding and application of his wise counseling.

Mrs. Helen Ellington, a beautiful member of the first Norfolk Search for God (S.F.G.) group, shared the story of her first time of meeting Mr. Cayce. During his lecture for their initial meeting, he stated that before an entity can formulate a question of one's soul desire for knowledge, the answer is already there. That seemed so absurd to her that she tuned him out as a teacher. As he personally bade each member adieu as they were leaving the event, he said, "Helen, when you get home and think of what I said, you will realize that God has provided, within your conscience, the answers for your questions. Allowing them to be awakened when you want to listen brings out the question." Realizing that he had read her mind was disconcerting, but true in assessment; she was thereafter his avid student.

For Gladys Davis, the fertile atmosphere of Mr. Cayce's kind nature and the graciousness of his wife, Gertrude, allowed her to thrive in her own personal development. Her wisdom in carefully organizing the Readings blossomed as the momentum of people's interest soared, expanding her role in helping others gain access to the Readings in addition to helping the Cayces. She undertook with typical "Gladness" a project which would survive Edgar and Gertrude's passing by over forty years as the Readings evolved from her shorthand notes, typed pages and carbon copies to microfiche, computers and the searchable databases of the Internet during the course of her lifetime.

Gladys had a knack for identifying special talents in individuals. Her "shorthand code" when introducing them to me was, "He (or she) was sent." I understood innately what she meant from our long association with the Work. Edgar Cayce had the same spontaneous sense of recognition, as did many of their early associates. That instinctive talent was prevalent among the cooperative founders of the Association for Research and Enlightenment and has accounted for the unique culture of its dedicated members and staff today.

Few men appear in leadership roles with more genteel awareness of the efficiency of their female staff as did Edgar Cayce. Because of his uniqueness of insight, steered by recognition of spiritualized strengths, he promoted their leadership skills. Just as Jesus utilized the dedication of women as teachers and caretakers, he never discounted their service to the cause. Choosing men who valued similar attributes in their family partnerships, he built an organization that honored the divine natures of all people, male, female, adults and children. The ego-adjustment in gender, race, class, age and social status was pooled in a mutual enrichment of spiritual attunement, rather than in a power-control status over others.

Edgar Cayce's humility was matched by the willingness of Gertrude and Gladys to sacrifice material comforts for spiritual assurance. Teaming their mutual encouragement ensured a balance in tenacity as they inspired groups which furthered their dedication in awakening humanity's need of spiritual guidance.

The courage of Edgar Cayce as he applied absolute Faith with each Reading was astounding. Being willing to lay aside his "self," or consciousness of existence, placing total trust in spiritual protection, just to seek aid for other humans who often were strangers was a test of Faith that so few of us would choose to exercise. Within about three minutes after lying down on the couch, he had released his self-awareness into a state of surrender, ready to be propelled into the realm of Wisdom that could answer the Quest for Knowledge for the seeker. That is the active principle of Christ Consciousness!

Explanations of the processes his psyche endured as it traveled through space in search of the Akashic Records to read the answers for the clients who sought them was fascinating. Sometimes he followed beams of light. Sometimes he was encapsulated in a bubble. I was intrigued by the Reading given that, as he laid aside his consciousness, his soul was placed in an "alabaster box" beside his somniloquistic body. Entrusting it to the conductor, some aspect of his intellectual awareness traveled through the ethers of time and space to locate the client-entity's records and translate what was allowed to be transmitted back through his trance-induced body, while awaiting his cue to return in healthy wholeness to retrieve his soul and awaken his body.

In contemplation of the challenge he faced to achieve each Reading, my mental image dramatized the scenario of Edgar Cayce, laying his individual ego aside. Armored in the brilliant humility of total trust in Grace-protection, his search for Truth used the sword of the Akashic Records to penetrate the wall of ignorance which blocks the path toward Enlightenment. Each quest required his life be held hostage as ransom until his return to consciousness.

When Gertrude became the Conductor, more positive results were assured for his health. She was not tempted to abuse his soul purpose as a healthy asset in his spiritual assistance. Partnership in attunement with both Gertrude and Gladys enhanced Edgar Cayce's faith, health and focus of dedication.

The Cayce family's concern for his welfare was stoically brave throughout all the health challenges they witnessed as he exceeded the scope of warnings about his overload. His ability to place others' needs before his own seems to have the quality Gladys shared equally as she dedicated her life to his service.

The benefits of human concerns are multiplied when groups unite, as we surely learned since the Essenes harmonized their hope and faith in preparing for the Messiah to enter Judea. Even as now, women initiated ties of mutual benefit in their community, establishing a harmonious atmosphere for sharing the work between the many families who dedicated their lives to ideals the Essene community chose to apply. Civility instilled in children, maintained through consistent discipline, enabled men to adhere to principles conducive to spiritual dedication. Maturing within such a protective consideration of one another strengthened their divine attributes of patience as they centered their hopes on the prophecy of the Messiah. Pharisees and Sadducees may have ranked higher in the Sanhedrin's governance of the Temple, but the Essenes produced the chosen channel for the Messiah through their powerful focus on hope and faith.

Women play a vital role today in spiritual dedication and in the influence of children by emphasizing their spiritual guidance of the conscience factors innate in all. While the hierarchical leadership of various Churches is dominated by male representatives, the groundwork is still laid by a strong feminine influence. In witness of the healing forces at work among our growing numbers of Search for God groups, women outnumber male participants. Vital to the success of Edgar Cayce's spiritual application was the understanding verification of the strong women on whom he depended for encouragement. Gertrude's stamina and astute practicality, enhanced by her experience in her past life as Socrates' daughter, armed her with an ideal capacity to provide the balance he needed through their constant challenges. As a wise wife and mother— and devoted mentor for Gladys, too—her influence has permeated every essence of the Work.

I had a sample of her inspiration every time Gladys joined me for lunch, dinner, or when our visits extended in either her home or mine. Especially dear to my recall were the personal chats when we could trigger excerpts from memory of previous excursions of our past lives. We recognized the patterns of repetitions in experience when our contacts were renewed with the same individuals that we had known before. Her adoration of Mrs. Cayce, her patience and mature advice spoke through the bonds I felt from our Persian experience. We knew no barriers in discussions of any subject that presented itself to us, no matter how personally it unfolded, trusting the ethics of our friendship. Every soul should be so blessed with a friend so trustworthy and non-judgmental. Understanding by mature friends is an exceptional blessing. She managed to view others in the light of their ideals and best intentions. Magnifying virtue, minimizing faults, and for those traits, she gave credit to those mentors, like Gertrude, whose patience had helped her in adjusting to the challenges she had faced through earlier years, especially the constant review and application of the Readings' timely advice.

Their community participation was thoroughly encompassing. Each member of the family found friendly connections with the residents at the Beach. They attended local churches, and Mr. Cayce was soon teaching a Sunday School class, while Search for God groups expanded from the original Norfolk membership. Healing was sought by many, and the Life Readings were increased. In maturity and evident readiness, God had sent his former assistant, the twin soul of their mission, Gladys Davis, to help in rejuvenating minds to recognize the pattern for soul perfection. Since their days together in Persia, Cayce had entered the Promised Land, where Jesus assigned him a missionary role. He later became the Bishop of Laodicea, where he helped to lead others to follow Jesus. Having fathered Zend, his psychic connection must have further inspired his ability to teach.

Through his and other Life Readings, Edgar Cayce reawakened to the roles he had experienced before, including the short French span as Gladys' son and the wanderings of a river boat gambler in an early American detour. Brought back on track, he reconnected with Gladys, Gertrude and Hugh Lynn as his major soul purpose was rediscovered. Vacations, even to the "other side" have merit, but Earth's "home-front" duties, tough as they may be, do reward one's commitment, especially when applied as his were.

God's Divine Pattern is designed to be executed through dedicated processes of spiritual attunement. Willing to experience the physical life through being Adam and many other lifetimes before culminating in His death and Resurrection as Jesus, Christ Consciousness was exemplified as a sustained awareness of God's Presence. Within the soul of every human embryo is the potential awareness of its purpose in sharing the Christos, (Light) vibration, and Spirit (Breath) of the Divine Source of Life-Itself. Edgar Cayce understood and taught this concept by word and deed.

Although the recorded data of history has detailed much of the experiences of the soul's challenges during His incarnations on the Earth plane as Adam, (Enoch, Melchisadek, Buddha, Zend, Joshua) and Jesus, miscalculations abound. Our "Oneness" as part of the whole is always the vital focus. The Vine, whose root is the Creator and Source of all Supply, laces through the arbors of every positive Theological approach of Divinity.

In a Reading (#281-59) given for the Healing Group, Cayce gave this purpose for Jesus' birth: "First, that the level of man's consciousness might be such that he, man, would be as aware of God as of himself. Second, as in each of His promises to man, that love might abound; that there would be a continued communion with God through the Son, who offered Himself as a means of man's approach to the Father." Message: "Lo, I am with thee always, even unto the end of the world." As Jesus expressed it, "I Am the Vine, and ye are the branches." The Vine grows and winds through many gardens of religious thought, from the highest peaks of Tibet to the shores of every sea. It is not exclusive to any culture, nor is the "Christos," or the enlightened consciousness of God, exclusive to Christianity. Semantics often interfere in understanding its ecumenical "Oneness."

Because God—as Love, Creator, Potter, Source—manifests Universal Beauty by populating our planet with cells of Life in His spiritual image, Creation is energizing Eternity through us. Universal Laws apply to all elements that exist. We are sustained as cells in the Body of God as parts of the whole being, whether aware of it or not. The wonder of such awareness is prevalent in our search for attunement, and the desire to share with others the understanding of its principles. The Readings awaken this awareness.

In the historical records of various religious factions, myths and traces of lost civilizations, God's Spirit has covered the gamut of all human experience.

This generosity overwhelms our capacity to realize or appreciate Agape Love of that magnitude. Abuses which threatened to annihilate the potential survival of humanity have been met with God's Grace. Willing to send as a Savior His most cherished Son, to save the errant souls, the altar of His sacrifice was prepared to show us how Love operates in our behalf. Freedom of choice and consequences that result over many lifetimes require time and space to understand Universal Law as it applies "an eye for an eye, a tooth for a tooth," or compensation for the "extra mile." "In patience, possess ye your souls," states Scripture, but often we misunderstand. The tragic events result as karmic law of choice.

We realize that God is not mocked when we fail to get our revenge NOW. In the patient fairness of His Sovereignty as Judge we can rely. The theory of reincarnation allows us to better understand how great God's Love and Patience truly are in generating the opportunity for each of us to Learn, to grow in Wisdom. Experience, good and bad, is our teacher. Mistakes must be corrected through recognition by ourselves. No one else can teach us. Sometimes, the only way that we can learn is through feeling such pain and suffering as that we caused others to experience. "Do unto others as you want to have done to yourself," is learned when the "shoe" is on our own foot. Our suffering is better understood by realizing it is a teacher, often resulting as payment for a debt of past choices. That is not always true, as the Good Book lists such exceptions as the blind Bartemaeus, lest we begin to "Judge" all the afflictions we see as "deserved" debts. Saints and sinners share our services through every incarnation. I like to think that within my own skin there is a bit of both potentials, as I count on God's patience with me.

The role of His Son as a sacrifice for humankind's sake is often mis-understood as being a "scape-goat" instead of as a Shepherd of the lambs of God, leading while protecting. In defense of our spiritual heritage, Jesus patterned the Way that all must follow. In allowing His soul to inhabit the clay model of Adam, He served as a guide through every avenue of physical experience, proving God's attributes worthy of power to overcome all obstacles. The Messiah interceded in our behalf that we might realize our true Spiritual identity. As individual cells in the body of God, through application of Righteousness (right use of His Agape Love), we, too, can follow the Prodigal Son's return to Everlasting Life. Repenting of self-willed use of time, space and energy is the price of fellowship in His Kingdom, as

I understand the composite of messages gleaned from the thousands of Readings given. Choosing to exchange "my will" for "Thy Will" out-performs any world market ever devised in multiplying our dividends mentally, physically and spiritually.

In studying Cayce's Life Readings, with their range of individual approaches to the Throne of Grace, each entity seeking advice was given three or four lifetime capsules of events that affected their choices of mental or spiritual growth with appraisals. Each was treated to answers within perimeters of their own understanding. Broad ecumenical values allowed a central core of unity across the spectrum of religious diversity, encouraging each to work within their scope of view. Although Edgar Cayce was an avid Christian, there was no derision of any major religious doctrine. Pathways to God seem to arrive at the harmony of Love, tolerance and deeds.

The Way is marked with many signs of instruction along its course so that every soul can eventually recognize its own Native Spirit and freely express it. God's patience prevails as we struggle to discern the required direction of our steps toward that enlightenment. Souls who have followed His footsteps closely throughout their existence have volunteered their services, returning as shepherds when sent by Him to guide the flock of strays. Edgar Cayce, Gertrude, Hugh Lynn and Gladys, in concert with a host of fellow disciples, have assumed a vital responsibility in leading those of us whose chosen paths merge in the fellowship of Christ Consciousness. Their schools are not exclusively the only courses being offered to the diverse cultures inhabiting this planet, but serve to enlighten students who choose to engage in applying this particular approach. Free Will allows each soul to pursue its chosen ideal and fate. Credit card debts do come due. One settles the bill by suffering or a change of will. Grace is FREE!!!

Multitudes of diversely interested souls have shared their approach to God via the messages received. Through Edgar Cayce's attunement in translating the Akashic Records and the efforts of Gladys Davis to preserve them, the benefits of the Readings now extend to all mankind, continuing their flow of influence through time and space. A river of knowledge supplies oceans of wisdom when the tenets of their doctrine are applied righteously, as prayer and study groups all over the world are proving daily.

Since Love is innate as our spiritual basis of existence, it is implanted in each core of our souls as our "Christ Consciousness." One would assume that expressing Love is instinctual. For most individuals, that is a natural emotion of Life's force. Alterations began as souls, when tested by deceit, chose selfishly. Before Reason as an analysis of experience was developed, motives such as desire presented temptations to the obedient through curiosity. Creative experiments negated loyalty to conscience by swaying emotions.

Whether self-satisfaction or self-glorification motivates the distraction, when conscience is outbid by the temptation of desire, the gate is opened for untamed horses to escape. Emotions of the physical world are the wild horses, eager to taste freedom from spiritual control. Stabilizing emotions are systemic, affecting the whole body. Adam and Eve's first-born son, Cain, inherited the systemic poison of emotional lack of control, jealously murdering his young brother, Abel, in envy of his spiritual attunement of God's favor. Trouble foreclosed Eden's property as Adam's abode, and human love has been confused by lack of trust ever since.

Patience of God, as Love Itself, in forgiving and long-suffering, allowed Adam to redeem control over self-indulgent will. His further reincarnations presented the opportunity to learn a respect for sharing Love through service. The process of God's generosity of Time and Space gave Him opportunity to grow in grace, suffering as all do, through the karmic experience of cause and effect, to the ultimate test. Willing total control of Self to God's Love, He surrendered physical life in behalf of humanity's soul. The Pattern established redemption and, through it, the promise of eternal life.

Even greater suffering than physical pains for Him was the Hell endured in the absorption of human hatred in its ignorance of compassion which cut the bonds of Life from its presence of Love. "WHY hast Thou forsaken me?" The serpent's lie of separation from God's existence is Hell for all souls who cannot sense the "Presence of Love." In the Resurrection, God gave the full recharge of Life, in approval of Jesus' sacrifice as the Pattern of compassion that offers hope of redemption for all of His children who will allow Love to guide their choices of future behavior. As a means of continuing spiritual contact after His ascension, the Holy Ghost as Universal Spirit is made available to answer all calls, relaying messages to and from Him. Our Dreams, as promised, can also provide direct service connections, if we keep the lines clear of disrupting static.

Jesus, in more than full measure, worked to restore man's obedience to God by mastering a Pattern of principles that inspires all followers of God's plan. As Master of ideal balance in applying the law of Oneness, over and over, the Readings refer to the Pattern, as imprinted in the mind's awareness of each entity, as called Christ Consciousness. The light switch is turned on when the choice to attune oneself to Christ's Pattern is made.

In fulfilling His potential, with God's approval, Jesus met the challenge for which He had volunteered. By allowing hate's crucifixion, through physical death in overcoming Satanic forces of fear, doubt and agonizing pain, He proved His total self-allegiance in trusting God's Will which empowered Life to be regenerated.

Resurrection served to open Death's door with the key of Love to all who obey the Law. By Loving God (Good) as our Source of All Supply and sharing His Love Supply with all of our neighbors, we, too, can share the Resurrection. His presence is available via heart, mind and soul, as we apply the desire to live according to His Will. Awareness of His presence is a choice by our invitation. Being aware that Love cannot be forced from an unwilling heart and soul, God knows it can only be expressed by choice. Service is the outlet from which it flows freely. No obligation is attached to pure love beyond a reflection of gratitude. In discerning the motivational source of Love, beware if you detect any strings attached.

The prodigal's return to the purity of Agape Love was a series of lessons, I gather from this study, each an effort to evict self-centeredness through practicing awareness of divine nature. As citizens of this planet, we are fellow prodigals on the path of reincarnating through Love's school of compassion, practicing our roles to appear on Heaven's stage, though not all are aware of its degree program. Edgar Cayce and Gladys Davis, supported by many stagehands, were well-chosen by The Producer to direct the students of the Association of Research and Enlightenment through their act of the Play. Learning our moves as we recite our lines has been like enjoying Sunshine on the Beach while we follow their examples.

Balancing contact with the members and board of trustees in keeping with the ideal aims of their association's thrust and budget with perspectives of personal attunement was a strain shared by all. Health and stamina dominated challenges of their accelerated course of dedication. Mr. Cayce's response to the needs of others, exceeded the limits of practical advice by jeopardizing his own physical health. Crowding into his daily schedule multiple Readings, when two per day had been prescribed as apropos when in ideal health, kept Gertrude and Gladys stressed. Their pleas were over-ruled by his sense of pressure to serve others' needs and his willing sacrifice of himself.

Practical caution had little room for consideration within his pressurized psyche, while his sons were ensnared in the trenches of World War II and so many families suffered likewise. Perceptions of being needed are powerful forces which often confuse the rigors of common sense in "givers." One's path is destined to follow its choice of will, distracted by none other than the Source of All Supply. When the will is aligned with the ideal of service, it follows the pattern Jesus expressed when He washed the feet of His disciples. Since Love is giving, only a receiver is required. Allowing the giver to express Love is reflective of appreciation, honoring the gift.

As many of Edgar Cayce's messages imply, God, the Giver, as exemplified by His son as servant, requires expression. All creative energy flows through channels for manifestation. Blocking its flow is frustrating the will of its

Law, as giver of Love Itself. Recognizing ourselves as channels through which His power flows significantly honors our spiritual identity. Our talents of service flow freely when powered by Love. Edgar Cayce, being so aware of himself as a channel of God, desiring as he did to be of help during this crucial period of stress in the world, could find no sanctuary for escape. He chose to sacrifice for the sake of others' needs, as he understood them, giving his life to the Cause.

Roanoke Retreat

Seeing that his health was declining, Gertrude and Gladys managed to convince Edgar Cayce to take time off for recuperation by going to Roanoke, Virginia, a community of the Blue Ridge hills. The added stress of world events and families' tragic losses kept his correspondence at the peak of

Mr. Cayce's agenda, even after his declining health forced them to cancel numerous Readings. His compassion for others knew no bounds as he sacrificed self-perseverance that others might find relief. In an effort to relieve his pressures of urgency to comply with the growing backlog of scheduled appointments, Gladys and Gertrude encouraged him to get away from the overcrowded headquarters to a hotel in the more relaxed mountain town of Roanoke. On September 17, 1944, he gave his last Reading, in seeking a health diagnosis for instructions to prolong his ability to serve others (294-212).

A week later, he suffered a stroke, and subsequent medications seemed to have an adverse effect. While there, he dictated a letter on October 19, 1944, to the Board of Trustees, expressing regret that he would not be present at their upcoming meeting, "Yet you know I am with you in spirit and purpose, when that purpose is to serve our fellow man in love, patience, long-suffering, bearing one another's burdens." In it, he requested, "At this time I am asking, and have asked, Miss Gladys to be my personal representative. She knows my personal wishes, as well as the faults and failures of each of us, as we have tried to be of a service through this channel. I do not feel that there are a great many drastic changes to be made just now, until Hugh Lynn can return to act as Manager of the Association, which we trust by His grace will be in not too distant future, I would like to have the Executive Committee appoint Miss Gladys as Treasurer," which made possible her ability to keep the accounts viable after his demise.

Treatments to renew his recovery efforts from a bout with a pulmonary virus proved fruitless. He managed to keep dictating letters to his sons and a few others, though. Edgar Evans was allowed a short leave to come home, so on Nov 21, 1944, he had an ambulance transport his father back to his beloved lakeside home in Virginia Beach. His joy of homecoming added improvements for his last Christmas and New Year's Day of 1945, before the release of his gracious soul on January 3.

Edgar Cayce and Gladys, Summer 1943.
Photo courtesy of the Edgar Cayce Foundation.

Gladys had always kept a daily record of events. Even during this period of dire circumstances affecting their personal relationships, she dutifully recorded each pertinent act. Mr. Cayce's physician had visited and, as he left, declared that nothing more could be done by him, leaving him in the care of God and his devoted wife.

Gladys accompanied the physician to the door as he expressed his condolences. Then, she climbed the stairs with reverent heart as she entered the room to begin her evening shift. She witnessed the endearing scene of Edgar's declaration of love to his wife, and Mrs. Cayce's response of mutual devotion to him before she headed downstairs for her solace and rest.

Shortly thereafter, Edgar Cayce's sister, who had been a constant source of help to Mrs. Cayce and herself since Mr. Cayce had come home from Roanoke, entered as Gladys noted in her diary:

> "6:30 P.M. Miss Annie Cayce brought him up some oyster stew, which he had known beforehand that she was making for him. He took 2-3 sips of it.
>
> 7:15 P.M. He stopped breathing."

Of all the duties that Gladys willingly performed, none could have been more emotionally exhausting, or as excruciatingly painful to record, than his demise. Grief's options of anxiety, or self-pity, could not be allowed to surface her consciousness. Sharing his loss, Gladys' first concern was Mrs. Cayce's fragile health requiring that she exhibit an empathetic mask of strength to support the team of volunteers and bereft staff. Surely, "Mister Cayce" would have counted on her to carry the banner of hope when he was forced to release it. She was designated to lead those left to move the troops forward. She could not flinch when duty fell in her lap.

Members of A.R.E having access to the total record of Edgar Cayce's Readings and her reports can read entire coverage of all the filed material. His funeral details are given and eulogies by numerous individuals and newspapers. Lists of authors of books and magazine articles would fill reams of paper since his transition January 3, 1945, thanks to Gladys' dedication to the Work.

Washington, D. C. 1944-45

World War II was such a horrible experience for my large family, and it seemed to go on forever. Employed at a "government job" in Washington, I lived there till after the war ended. All my brothers had returned in 1945 from Europe, in dread of being sent to Japan. Spared from that ordeal were millions of service men like them when Japan finally surrendered.

As I walked down 16th Street to work one morning in 1944, Vice President Harry Truman joined me. He began a very friendly conversation that day which initiated a daily routine. Being of the age and similar coloring of his daughter, Margaret, I probably tempted him to find out what her peers were thinking. Since my Dad was quite similar in frame and also farm-faced, our first conversations were congenially philosophical in quality, especially so when he learned that I was a Theology and parapsychology student. However, President Roosevelt's death in 1945 altered his routine "constitutionals," as he called his early morning walks. As the fates would have it, Margaret and I sold war bonds and books of stamps via U.S.O. floats, and I enjoyed sharing her family at Blair House while The White House was being renovated.

I left D.C. in the spring of 1946 as the cherry blossoms adorned the nation's capitol. The irony of such beauty, the gift of an earlier Japan, whose act of war, December 7, 1941, had loosed the fires of Hades to rain upon them such a devastating destruction, exemplifying War as Hell on Earth. Even now, there is no more horrible scene of inhumane behavior, yet Man has not seemed to learn to avoid such conflict. The threat of worse violence still haunts our human survival. That is inconceivably irrational for me to digest.

When, years later, I learned of Edgar Cayce's services in D.C., the psychic phase of his participation touched special areas of interest for me, having spent those years in such close proximity to the White House. Mr. Cayce's special consultations with World Affairs was kept so quiet during that era, while Hugh Lynn served with the Special Forces and Edgar Evans with the Army's Radar development. All of the Cayces paid heavy tolls for their war efforts. The pressures Edgar Cayce endured, feeling the anxieties that permeated the concerns of those families whose lives were affected while his urges to give comfort could only answer a small percentage of the need, must have been excruciating. Psychic sensitivities with his intense desire to serve as God's assistant allowed him no adequate rest during that war, I am sure.

References to his frequent quotes, such as "Man's search for truth is his search for God," are quite profound. None of his prophesies of future earth changes, and there are many, do I find more intriguing than that he gave in answer to the questions posed by an individual who asked if the prophecy made in May, 1941, that the war in Germany would end in the spring of 1944 was still possible. Here is an excerpt of the follow-up Reading:

TEXT OF READING 257-254 M 50 (Sales Mgr., Hebrew)

This psychic reading given by Edgar Cayce at the office of the Association, Arctic Crescent, Virginia Beach, Va., this 18th day of December, 1943, in accordance with request made by Mr. [257], Active Member of the Association for Research and Enlightenment, Inc.

47.(Q) Is the prophecy still possible of fulfillment, of May, 1941, that war against Germany will end in the spring of '44?

(A) This will end in the spring of '44. [3/57 GD's note: The 1950 World Almanac indicates that Hitler was wounded in an attempted assassination July 20, 1944. It is possible that this planned assassination was seen. If it had gone through, war would have ended immediately, long before the invasion.]

48.(Q) When will the war with Japan end?

(A) It will be much later, but more sudden in its close. [First atomic bomb was dropped on Japan August 6, 1945, the second atomic bomb was dropped August 9, 1945. Japan surrendered August 14, 1945.]

The book, *"Starling in the White House,"* covered that era when Mr. Cayce was invited to share Readings and insight there. Written by the author of *"There Is A River"* and the birthday greeting poem used to introduce our affection for Gladys, Thomas Sugrue had been Hugh Lynn's roommate at Washington and Lee University. He endeared himself to Edgar

Cayce, Gertrude, Gladys and T.J. as they shared years of togetherness, much of that period during the war. He was extremely helpful to Gladys and was one of her favorite people. His many articles, lectures, Readings and their memories of him shared by Gladys and T.J. convinced me that he would easily have been one of mine, too. His daughter, Patsy Channon, inherited his charm. Her mother, Mary, shared one of their audio tapes of Edgar Cayce's Readings, when the Archangel Michael spoke through him. Hugh Lynn presented it while addressing the audience attending the Easter 1975 Dedication Services of the new Library, or Visitors Center. A copy is on file in the archives of A.R.E.

Hugh Lynn, Gertrude, Edgar
Evans and Edgar Cayce in front
of their home on Arctic Circle.

PART TWO

Grief and Renewal

With the loss of Edgar Cayce, A.R.E.'s future seemed to be in jeopardy. The war was not yet over. Both of his sons remained in service of America's war effort. Preparations had been made earlier to sustain the organization as its membership grew; however, the staff faced decisions unparalleled in its history following his death. Gladys, as appointed by Mr. Cayce, became his representative. With the weight of his approval, through the Board of Trustees, it was determined A.R.E. would continue to function until Hugh Lynn could return. Notifying the membership and cancellation of all scheduled Readings for two years into the future was an immediate priority for Gladys and her staff following Mr. Cayce's burial.

Attentive care of Mrs. Cayce through her grief was shared by Gladys and the family's many devoted friends. Exactly three months after her beloved husband's transition, Gertrude passed away on Easter, leaving Gladys in charge of their grief-laden followers. Determined to keep the Association afloat until the world could again experience peace and both sons could return home, Gladys and the A.R.E. staff held tightly together, sharing the necessary duties as a new era began.

Surrounded by the grieving friends and local members of the prayer and meditation groups, Gladys had the willing support of volunteers. Lydia J. Schraeder Gray came to aid in notifying members and returning fees for scheduled Readings, basically taking charge of the household management. She remained in that capacity, superintending the care of the facilities at headquarters for decades while residing there.

Gladys tackled the challenges of saving the files from Harm

When Gladys returned to Virginia Beach from the funeral, the job of notifying all those with scheduled appointments of their cancellations and returning their pre-paid funds was Gladys' most pressing responsibility. She had prepared her lists while traveling, since she had taken those records to work on with her. Noticing that the filing cabinet containing the original carbons of the Readings was missing from its allotted space greatly disturbed Gladys upon her return, but the priority lists took precedence as a duty. Panic must be forestalled, she convinced herself, although inwardly she was deeply concerned. If just for Gertrude's sake, she had to appear calm. She began searching every room in anxious silence every chance she got a break from the tasks at hand.

Trying to hide her anxiety about the missing records from the ill and grief-stricken Mrs. Cayce, she finally went out to the woodshed to cry. As she neared the shed, the tears overflowed and the sobs began to shake her whole being. Under cover of the shelter, she was ready to flop on the stack of wood and allow herself the emotional release that she had harnessed since Mr. Cayce's demise. The flurry of a scampering rat startled her, as she strained to view through the blur of tears. BEHOLD! There lay the strewn ruins of the battered cabinet and her treasured carbon copies of his legacy. Her heart leaped with joy! Discovering that the old filing cabinet had not been stolen, but just trashed, renewed Hope. No more tears today, there was a more pressing job to do!

For reasons that he must have thought helpful, Harmon Bro, Ph.D., had dumped the wooden cabinet of carbon file copies on the shed-covered woodpile while Gertrude and Gladys were away in Kentucky attending Mr. Cayce's burial. But Gladys had found the treasured remains. Hallelujah! All was not lost, after all! Tenaciously gathering the cluttered scraps of wood and papers, though stained by urine, feces, balls of rat hair and chewed up copies of those precious Readings, her job was decidedly unique. Only Gladys could have saved the identical words that expressed the original messages as vocalized by Edgar Cayce. Thankfully, she had the foresight to save all of her shorthand steno pads over the years from which she could accurately reconstruct each page. Retyping each Reading, repairing the cabinet, she managed to keep her attitude of Gladitude aloft. Uncomplaining as was her nature by that point of her life, she diligently put the files back in order. Completing the job was her rewarding satisfaction. Through such opportunities as this she earned her sainthood, probably.

The shorthand of Gladys Davis.
Courtesy of the Edgar Cayce Foundation.

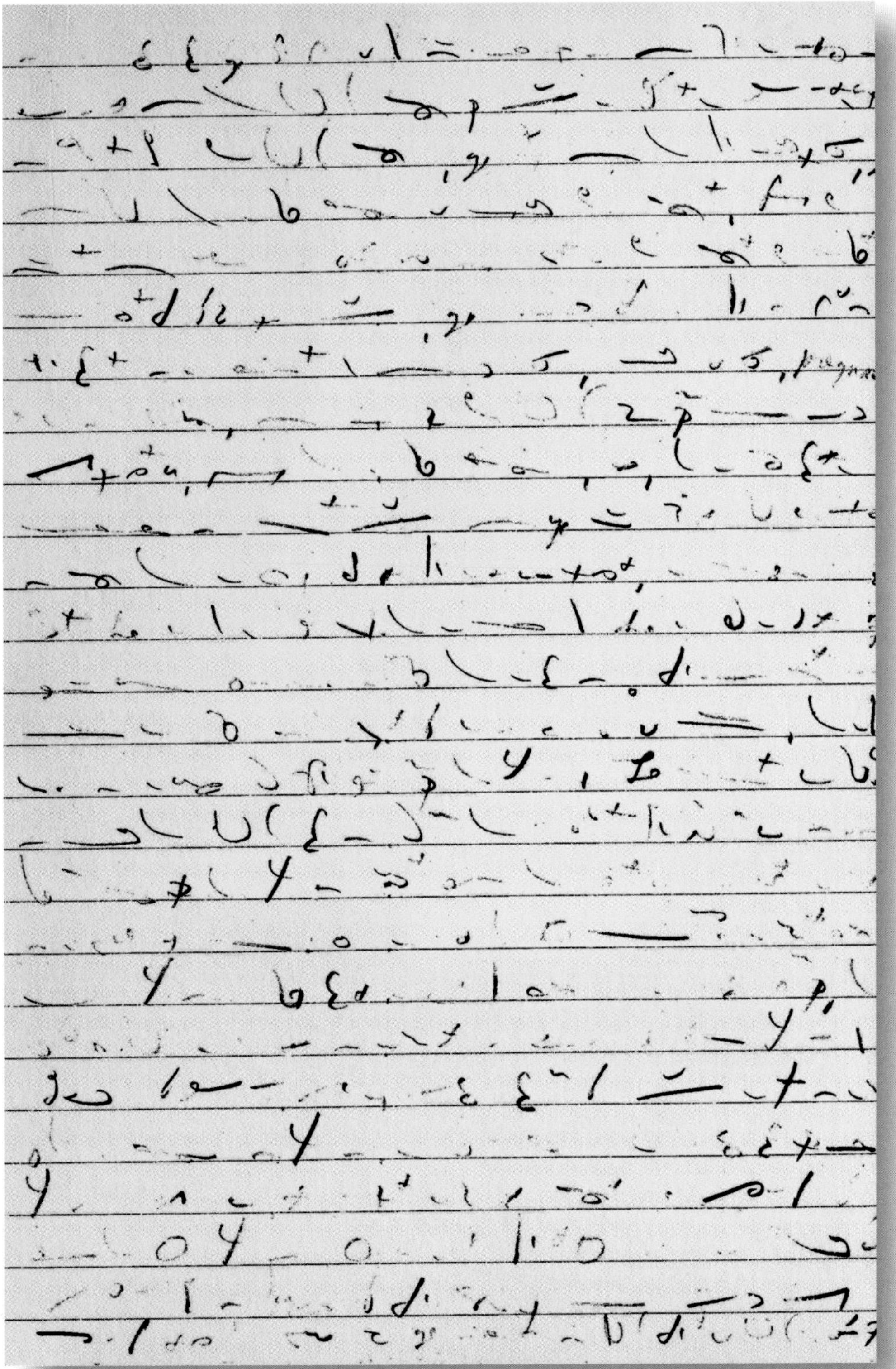

Shortly after completion of renewing her files, Harmon Bro came by to announce that he was heading for the train station in Norfolk to meet a representative from Dr. J. B. Rhine's parapsychology team from Duke University of Durham, N.C. He had taken it upon himself to initiate a deal for their emissary to look through the files, as a pre-sale evaluation of their potential worth to their team's research. Years before, Edgar Cayce had been the victim of their "scientific study abuses" when they, with others, were allowed to "observe" a session of "psychic trance" phenomena. Taking advantage of his "deep meditative state" they had probed his body with bacteria-laden tools of torture from which infections plagued him for months. That, Gladys still remembered so well. Harmon would be bringing the man back soon. She shuddered.

Forewarned, Gladys prepared for the next challenge. Placing all records in the wooden cabinet, she locked it with its only key. Then, quickly, she deftly dropped the key out of sight. On their arrival, she joined the group as they searched in vain for the missing key. Dedicated volunteers and employed Staff workers joined in the search of every nook and cranny of the home that served as Headquarters for A.R.E. Without a thorough perusal of the file contents, the man from Durham refused to dicker with Harmon about a sale price. When they finally rode away to catch the train returning him to North Carolina, neither man appeared very congenial.

When it seemed safe to do so, Gladys happily retrieved the key from her ample bra. Hugging the cabinet that she had so recently reassembled with its treasure of restored priceless records, she opened its drawers and resumed her duties in prayerful gratitude for their salvation—and her own.

There were other episodes requiring her firm stand on controlling the records. David Kahn, a long-time friend and supporting Trustee of A.R.E.'s Board, wanted to sell the files to a Harvard University group of researchers, so Gladys requested a promise from Hugh Lynn that he would agree to hold them until she received directions from his departed father. They made a pact, allowing time for his return to Virginia Beach and the delivery of Edgar Cayce's "directions" for their application. Guarding the file copies closely, she waited for Hugh Lynn's return from Europe.

So, the files were kept intact until Hugh Lynn returned from the War, when, together, they could execute the plan for the ideal use of all the records. Had Gladys been just a great secretary, her job would have ended when her salary did, which occurred on a number of occasions during those lean years. Without her continued dedication to the mission she shared with Edgar Cayce, we would have been denied the past 79-80 years of the Association for Research and Enlightenment.

This Work was her True Niche

Gladys Davis worked with Edgar Cayce from 1923 to 1945. At the time of his death, she had spent over half her 41 years in his service. Twenty-two years as secretary to the Seer of the Twentieth Century, followed by forty-one years dedicated to preserving the legacy of his gift for scholars' study and evaluation, her life exemplified the application of the tenets of the Readings she so fiercely fought to protect. Repetitious mental focus from dictation, transcription, copying, filing, retrieving, sharing discussions, vocal and in print, her mind became a living catalog of his psychic revelations. As the Readings emphasized that "mind is the builder," the fruits of spiritual development matured with her consistent service to kindred souls.

Neither Edgar Cayce nor Gladys had chosen their employment for its financial profits, prestige, comfort or luxurious vacations. Exercising their commitment to its rewards meant total loyalty to their Spiritual employer of body, mind and soul. No worldly scale of values distracted their aims of service in sharing their guidance with the masses of seekers.

With the demise of both Mr. and Mrs. Cayce preceding the end of World War II, while both of their sons were absent from home, Gladys' sense of responsibility remained attuned to faithfully pursuing her soul mission. As glue, in rallying those dedicated souls bonding into a community of healing forces to remain united, her role was as vital as the keystone in their arched gateway of existence. Her innate humility in service enabled the diverse egos to adhere in harmony with Gladness.

Gladys added those forty-one more years after the final Reading to set the records in order, so their merit for reference and research could be accessed by all interested in applying their potential therapy. Mr. Cayce had planted the flag on the Moon's surface, so to speak, proving its access plausibly within reach of humankind. Bringing his legacy to the World's awareness multiplied the value of his talents by millions of souls. Gladys' foresight and

Gladys in her office at
A.R.E. Headquarters, 1950.
Photo courtesy of the
Edgar Cayce Foundation.

tenacity validate her role as an equal partner in the life mission of Edgar Cayce and the Work. I think it is high time to give her public recognition for all the trials and private tribulations so few knew about. She covered so well and made her job look so simple. Guardian angels, such as herself, seldom exercise boastful pride. It is up to us to applaud her contribution.

Over and over she typed the words of the Readings which express the reasons for our incarnations. Each purpose gives adequate opportunities to prepare an indwelling of each soul with the will of a living God. "My spirit bears witness with thy spirit," as God-consciousness manifests through the choice of the soul.

Knowledge and understanding are havens of peace when applied. Growing in grace is the reflection of the indwelling wisdom of God within self as the soul reaches through willing attunement to share companionship with an Eternal Heaven. God is the source of Perfection, of Life, Love, Light and all Creation, where Universal Laws of order, abundance, joy and peace rule. As heirs of Divine Spiritual heritage, each of us has a claim on its wealth when we have learned to apply the principles set by obedience to its Laws. Avoiding that application of Life force merits the separation from Light (or Enlightenment), which is the damnation of Hell. Its pathway is found in the denial of Good in creating the spiritual fruits of Love's Presence in all our relationships.

Long ago, Edgar Cayce and Gladys Davis accepted their roles as Ambassadors to remind our generation of the Universal Laws and encourage us to master application of the tenets of behavior set by God's Son. Their words offer Hope that lessons of each lifetime experience can bring us nearer to Heaven's Gate with a permanent passport for citizenship. We are challenged to extend our reach to touch the benefits of their sacrifices in our behalf. They willingly served so that we could enhance Gladness in our own lives. Their brilliant spirits still communicate through mutually sharing the Work of the Christos.

Although the prospect of future Readings was gone, there was still much work to be done as Gladys assumed her next mission in continuing the Work. By the time of Hugh Lynn's return to civilian life, she was able to present him with her well-planned list. The faithful personnel cooperated admirably in readjusting to execute the organization's plan of preserving the Readings and making them available to the rest of the world.

With the return of Hugh Lynn, especially, they realized the value of sharing the entire collection of individual Readings as a helpful tool for practitioners and seekers. The Search For God groups had proven their merit. The prayer and meditation groups were so beneficial to the members and their communities that their outreach revealed a self-sustaining promise of hope. The vast knowledge contained in the Readings would benefit generations to come.

Hugh Lynn and Gladys cooperated to lay the foundation of the path to bring Edgar Cayce's recorded treasure of expertise to the public. Preparing the Readings for research and study was a labor-intensive operation for both of them as they designed the framework to organize a collection numbering in the tens of thousands of pages. They developed a numbering system to code individual readings and protect the identities of the recipients. Pooling health ailments, causes and therapeutic advice in categorical initiatives began an endless process of distinguishing research potential. Identifying former historical reincarnations, places and events were among other potential avenues of investigation. Their plans were met with encouragement and support from the membership as the rolls swelled with newcomers.

Now, with the void of personal contact with Gertrude and Edgar, Gladys felt a loneliness in the lack of their guidance. Granted, connections of fellow workers at headquarters, the challenges of organizing the Work, staff supervision and the responsibilities of decisions to be creative in planning ahead supplied ample contact with people. Every day the numbers multiplied the population of contacts with little time for personal concentration. Each evening, sorting concerns with no one mutually aware of the overload, no feedback suggestions of sympathetic understanding, she sensed the power of the proverbial black hole. Self-pity was not her calling, communication was. Seeing her "brothers," Hugh Lynn and Edgar Evans, back home at last with their wives and children was a joy to behold, yet a mirror that reflected her solitude.

Her mind reached for her own familiar messages, (#288-1) "One, who, with others, will draw much of the more beautiful things of the earth plane about them, one to whom all obstacles become stepping stones." She forced the thoughtful response necessary, "Thank you, Lord, for giving me the privacy I need, without any hassle, so that I can face all who require my assistance tomorrow. Smiling at the ironies of life is a facelift that beats washing my face in tears." Already, her stepping stones bore a resemblance to a stairway to Heaven's Gate.

Gladys had managed to assist her mother through the difficult years after her father's death, so that her brothers and sisters could finish school and acquire jobs and families of their own. Most of them were drawn to Virginia where her family bonds included nieces and nephews dear to her heart.

So, only after both Cayces had died and the legacy of their contribution to the Association for Research and Enlightenment was well-established, did Gladys, after 40 years as Temple Virgin, consider marriage. Albert Turner, a New York stockbroker, whose interest in verifying an intuitive pursuit of his own past lives through a series of hypnotic revelations, eventually won her affections and hand in marriage. Because of her dedication to the Work, he chose to leave Wall Street behind and move to Virginia Beach to make their relationship possible; thus, Al joined the ranks of its dedicated participants and Gladys became his bride.

Meanwhile, both Cayce brothers added children, and Gladys' siblings were adding to the family members moving nearer to her. Her nephew, Thomas Jefferson Davis, had grown up, and after an enlistment in the Marines and college abroad, married and gave her the chance of tasting the role of "Granny" with his son, Michael. She thoroughly enjoyed all of her nieces, nephews and their friends. Family life and the Work fulfilled her willingness to share the "Sunshine Gladness" of her nature. As her Readings had prophesied, she found her greatest joy in that role.

Gladys was so dedicated to her mission, yet seemed so naively innocent. Her soul memories retained impressions of various past lives, where scars of abuses that she had endured activated an alarm-alert system set to warn her of danger on sight of certain sharp implements. Her gender wariness stemmed from the vague impression that left traces of memory from her French lifetime when Edgar Cayce was her son who died before he was seven years of age. Her Reading gave some details of it, and his did, too. Then Al's later sessions of hypnosis seemed to add further explanations of the same tragic escapade. That lingering wariness probably spared her of relationships that normally endanger less careful young lovers. Being overly cautious, she avoided the possibility of repeating a similar event by consistently resisting the single-dating practices of her peers, preferring to be with groups of friends.

Missing many nuances of youthful flirting, the understanding of signals that differentiate the roguish tendencies of promiscuous philanderers was foreign to her, even as a mature woman. She had adapted a version of seeing an ideal of goodness in others and basically overcame most of her former fears of potential physical and emotional abuse. Working under standard cultural protocol, she mastered the art of soothing the beasts of innate incivility in her associates, but kept a safe distance away.

Rather than have a family of her own, she had focused more intently on her skills of service to others, devoutly bestowed through platonic relationships. Inadvertent as her sacrifice may have been, we are the beneficiaries of her devotion of time and energies dedicated to absorbing every essence of Mr. Cayce's messages. Had she allowed the distraction of bearing children to interrupt her attention from the phenomena of listening to God's words as Cayce vocalized them, her voracious absorption of them may never have developed and their messages silenced for the masses.

Her marriage to Al came after his convincing her that in the French lifetime he did not abandon her intentionally. Al took an active role in A.R.E. study programs, as he had been involved for years in seeking greater understanding of his own past lives. Gladys believed that she had shared past lives with him before and, although his health was a big challenge for years, their marriage lasted sixteen years.

Al's niece, Carol Baraff, generously presented me with books written about his past lifetimes that were revealed during a series of sessions with a hypnotist of that period. Each session was audio-taped and eventually transcribed by Carol's cousin, Doris Patterson, who worked as a secretary for Gladys during that era. Her books about *"The Man with Nine Lives"* and *"Beautiful Dreamer"* provided illuminating details of his past which coincided with the Life Readings that Edgar Cayce had given Gladys. The French experience matched, with Al's sessions adding details as to the reasons that their marriage was not allowed to legalize her son's paternity. Having traveled to England during his courtship with the teen-aged Gladys in that lifetime, he was not allowed to return to France as her husband and legitimate father of her son (Edgar Cayce, as Readings for Gladys [#288] and his own Reading [#294] identified him).

Within Al's hypnosis records, references that identified Gladys seem recognizable, though not all were among the few that Edgar Cayce referenced in his Readings for her. The French lifetime, mentioned in both, dovetailed in details, uniquely updating Al as the Duke of York, the young lover whose exit left Gladys as the unwed mother of a son, whom Edgar Cayce had identified as himself. Al's hypnotist recorded Al's experience of being detained against his will in England, as he desperately attempted to return to France. Their tragic circumstances left Gladys with a deep mistrust of men that her soul memory brought into this twentieth century, possibly aiding her resistance to marriage until he, as the specific culprit, convinced her of his sincere devotion.

When she and I discussed this lifetime and Al's re-encounter, she stated that his concerted efforts to convince her of his commitment were required. She clarified her long-carried distrust of men, having known no previous accounting for his abandonment. The repercussions resulting from giving birth to his son, Dale (Edgar Cayce, #294), who became a "threat of jealousy" to the ruler of France caused her life, and his, to be tragically cut short. Such events scar memories borne by the soul which heal slowly.

During Edgar Cayce's Egyptian life as Ra-Ta, Gladys, as his offspring via Isis (Gertrude, #538), suffered an early demise after being abandoned by the forced exile of her parents. Facing abandonment has a debilitating effect on one's attitude for survival. It is universal by nature of the will's choice.

The political situation and jealous anxieties of power that played such a devastating effect on all of their relationships is an interesting key when trying to understand the intricacies of reincarnation, especially of twin souls. A Reading requested by Edgar Cayce (#294-9) gives an in-depth explanation of the relationship of Gladys and himself, placing emphasis on the spiritual aspects instead of the physical, as most humans are more likely to do.

Long after Al's death, I had asked her if she had experienced any dream visitations by him that verified his continued awareness of her life. She gladly gave a detailed report of her extended wait. Al had died during A.R.E. Congress week of June, 1968, and his memorial service was attended by most of us who knew him. Her attention to all the events, people, messages and settlement of estate records kept her involved for an extended period as she anticipated his visitation from the other side. As the summer passed and autumn, too, she assumed that he was planning to join her during the Christmas Holidays in some surprising way. When New Years passed with no message yet delivered that carried his signature, she sat down and gave herself a lecture. She must apply her full attention to the Work which she felt was suffering because of the nagging distraction in her anticipation of soul communication with her departed husband.

Prayers, meditations and the constant exchange of supporting friends and family fueled her sense of well-being. Then, on the night of January 29, with the bells still peeling the midnight hour, Al appeared in her dream. "Happy Birthday!!!" Now that was his signature salutation, just as it had always been his greeting to everyone, friend or stranger, everyday, while living in Virginia Beach. Having given up the waiting game after more than six months, his visit was a birthday surprise, a reminder in harmony with his own natural expression.

True to her nature, on the night Gladys died, I was awakened by sensing her hand on my shoulder. Jeanette Thomas, her assistant, had called within minutes of her transition, and I had spent hours in "Gladitude,"

searching Scripture for consolation. When I first felt her touch, I sensed her compassion for my loss, but lay there in semi-slumber. Then, her hand gently shook me. As I rose up from my pillow, the room was aglow. Surrounded in a brilliance so dazzling that my sleepy eyes could not distinguish her facial features, she managed to communicate her thoughtful concern for me. "I didn't want you to have to wait." That's the Gladys I knew! Always, "others" mattered most!

Although years had passed since Al's demise, I understood instantly that she knew I would anticipate her visit in the months ahead. Her concern for others reminded me of Jesus' awaiting Mary Magdalene's visit to his empty tomb, to assure her that he was alive in Spirit and Truth. Not that I had any doubt about Gladys' whereabouts, but her thoughtfulness was reassuring, as everlasting. I called Mildred Davis the next day to share the details of her transition.

Al's sessions under hypnosis offered other examples of possible lives that may have included Gladys, although not mentioned in the few that were given by Edgar Cayce. His own Reading (#294-9) contains a reference to her.

"These two have ever been together, you see, except in the American forces when there was the soon return in that of the wanderer, and in the Grecian [Trojan] period." Each time, this entity, Gracia, or Gladys [#288] as known in the present, has been in the earth plane, so has Edgar Cayce [#294], as given in the series of her lifetimes. During Cayce's life as Lucius, during the time of Jesus and thereafter, Gladys did not enter, but served as his guardian from the "other side." In many notes that she added to the Reports that accompany the Readings, she expressed her own feelings about these subjects, verifying the validity, or not.

From 1923-1945 Gladys had served as Edgar Cayce's secretary until his death, then dedicated the remaining years of her life to the work he had undertaken. Preserving the Readings and noting the results of their use through continued contact with clients and their families, she archived his historical record, unmatched by any other psychic seer.

Marrying Al in 1952 at forty years of age did not faze her commitment to pursuing the goals that she had set in coordinating the pertinent details of each case history. Continued activity involving routines of balancing prayer, meditation, physical therapies as needed and a healthy diet as directed, she performed religiously, following directions of his Readings.

After Al's death in June, 1968, Gladys continued her full-time work of organizing the archived collection of pertinent records that lent credence to historical association of all whose past lives were involved. Following up on the results of recommendations for treatments, or prophecy fulfillment, she expanded inclusions that she knew could possibly aid future researchers and scholars.

During this period of establishing a foundation for the research and enlightenment of their generations—ours, and those yet unborn—the Cayce and Davis families endured trials and tribulations that are difficult for us to imagine. The "Cayce Home" headquarters had long ago been sold and occupied by other families through the ensuing years, but was finally bought by the Catholic Diocese to expand the activities of The Star of the Sea. To make way for a new playground, the house was scheduled to be demolished. It was decided to burn the structure to the ground as a training session for the firefighters from the Fire Department of Virginia Beach. The occasion was especially challenging for Gladys and her nephew, T.J., to experience.

T.J. told me about his memory of their shared poignant grief. In a meditative sadness the two sat together under an old fig tree in Gladys' yard, watching the flames consume the structure that had sheltered their existence through their formative years. Parading through their joint memories, Edgar and Gertrude Cayce led the procession of people whose lives had left indelible influence on both souls and all who knew them. Their spiritual links of inspiration had fused a web of concepts that would continue to enlace the world. Like the billowing smoke being incorporated within the ocean breezes, lifting it into the atmospheric blanket, their essence continues to permeate the planet—yea, the universe.

Probably, no other living individuals could have known the depth of mixed emotions that touched the hearts of those two souls, whose bonds of reincarnation tied them more closely with Edgar, Gertrude and their "Cayce Home." So many memories were reignited as they observed the flames reduce the edifice to embers.

Widowhood was a lonely experience for Gladys, even though her work schedule kept her in contact with so many friends and interesting contacts. Lovable and intelligent as she was, the dignity of her bearing gave her a distinction that belied her hunger for human companionship. From afar, potential partners, intimidated by her regality, dared not dream of seeking her affection.

During that phase of her life, I was invited to stay at the home of a mutual friend on the beachfront, including my friend, Betty, from Charlottesville. She came through Richmond and, from there, we traveled in her car. As a redhead, I shied away from the sunny beach during the day, preferring to sit in the library copying from the Readings. To do this, Betty dropped me off there, and she was due to pick me up later in the afternoon.

In 1956, the Old Hospital Building had been reacquired by the A.R.E. I sat in the Library there, copying by hand excerpts of various Readings for a few hours. At that time, there were no Xerox copiers yet available, so research was slow. The data would be typed at home on a manual type-writers later. Most of A.R.E.'s earlier authors had brought forth books and articles through this cumbersome method, which seems, by today's technological advances, to be of a prehistoric age.

Gladys had scheduled plans to meet Jess Stern at the Norfolk airport to drive him to his reserved hotel room on the Atlantic shore of Virginia Beach. He was producing a book about Edgar Cayce with the aid of her research staff (*"Sleeping Prophet"*). She was anticipating its public approval in an expanding awareness of Mr. Cayce's merits. Their association had been congenial in linking many mutual friends of the New York area with Edgar Cayce's notoriety. I knew a few of his intimate friends across the country and the general reputation of the man, but had never discussed him with Gladys.

On her way back to the Beach, she asked him if he could spare the time to drop by Virginia's place to meet one of her close friends. He agreed that it was a pleasure to meet any friend of hers. She evidently gave him a glowing verbal portrait of me, as a decade or so younger, adding enough details that set up a misconception in his fertile ego. Blind to her emotional attraction to him, he had assumed that she was playing "match-maker" for his egocentric nature. Arriving as a surprise at Virginia's door, they were welcomed by the ladies, who found the famous novelist so attractive that Betty, a recent widow, completely forgot that I was waiting for her to pick me up. Time passed for them so pleasantly as they waited for my arrival. Jess was enjoying the lavish adoration, and Gladys was relishing a rare social opportunity in sharing his charm with her friends. Only Gladys grew concerned by my delay. As I stood outside A.R.E.'s hilltop edifice, my anxiety grew in concern of Betty's traffic challenges. Finally I agreed to a friend's offer to transport me to the beachfront home.

Gladys beamed with animated joy as she introduced me to Jess, as she watched his effervescent approval. My heart sank as I ruefully soaked in the situation. She was as hyper as an infatuated teenager, and his obvious appraisal was spurred by having misconstrued her intentions for setting up our encounter. She had failed to identify my marriage status, and both were unaware that I was acquainted with his paramour, a decade or so my junior, who was sharing his "pad" in California at the time.

Gladys had wanted my evaluation of him as a candidate for her affection. It was among the most difficult situations of our friendship in which I found myself involved. I knew she would later ask my impressions of him. He had graciously invited Virginia and her houseguests to join him for breakfast at the hotel within a block of her home. She and Betty had agreed, and I dared not express my concerns with them. His attention to me I found easy to deflect, as I referred to my husband and children repeatedly in the morning conversation, so as to correct his misconceptions. Advancing a dialogue on the interests of writing, I used our research of the Cayce Readings as our mutual focus. Since I was working on a manuscript at A.R.E., he offered to share his agent for anything I wanted published, on the basis of Gladys' praise of my expertise. I managed to pass through the breakfast ordeal without creating an enemy of him.

Meeting Gladys later was a greater dread of diplomacy, since my heart ached for her, and I wanted to let her down to earth as easily as possible. Wishing to give her insight of Jess' playboy nature that blinded his capacity to recognize her value as a partner, I deemed him too shallow to be worthy of her littlest toe. I did not let her vocalize her feelings, avoiding her need to defend his attributes.

Using my "sister" role, I leapfrogged into a humorous tale of seeing him as a clown with a sad streak of blindness to virtue, rattled by some raunchy crudeness of a pedophiliac affliction to younger generations of his adoring fans before she had a chance to ask my opinion. Pretending that I did not see her blushing glow of attraction for him, I managed to introduce a new perspective for her to consider first. Confusing her, I felt like a snake in the grass. She soberly stated that she felt that she had known him before. I agreed that he was probably a jester in French courts when she was too young to recognize a rogue.

Her delayed experience with physical passions in remaining a virgin past the age of forty had only reinforced her naïve approach to sexuality, even into widowhood. Such a dilemma seems improbable to the worldly-wise of our generation. However, she was not of this world, and her adjustment was phenomenally painful to watch.

Years after Gladys died, Jess was expressing to me some disgruntled views of concerns he felt at the time: "Micki, A.R.E. used to be operated by giants, and now, it's being run by pygmies." Lacking Gladys' ability to only see the positive in people, I was cynical enough to be thinking that he should be quite happy to communicate with fellow pygmies. I kicked myself as I remembered the phrase, "It takes one to know one," whenever we choose to label others. *Mea culpa.*

Near Death Experiences

While crossing the threshold of youth into adulthood, I was welcomed into Ethereal Light through a near death experience. In 1946, such events were not topics of casual conversation. In the field of medicine where I worked, my survival context was considered rare, and even miraculous. Mystified colleagues did an anatomical survey of my revived corpse, but a fearful caution of being considered insane prevented any open discussion of my state of consciousness.

Weeks later, the opportunity to share a philosophical evaluation with my father allowed me to reveal the details of my exit from the restrictions of physical life at age 21. Describing the preliminary events, I then launched into the process of sensations that I felt as the physical life forces shut down all vibrations, gradually releasing me from my body's extremities and vital organs. I was aware of being, as a spark of light, moving into Light Itself. Free as the air released from a balloon, expanding, fusing with sheer ecstasy of Being, yet aware of my distinct individuality within it, I was filled with the ecstasy of Light Itself, Life's vibration at a degree that the physical body could not possibly sustain. For such an experience, the soul has to be released from the constraints of its physical limits.

Dad's words detailed the same sequenced process, verifying the pattern, so that he understood exactly what I was trying to express. "You've been there, too, Dad, but when?"

"When I was your age, I had such an experience. My father, too," so he finished the tale. "I thought I'd do you the same favor. Throughout the ages, God has used this method of enlightening individuals, to better prepare them for their mission in life. While out of the body, I'm sure you received further instructions, as God did for me and my Dad." Somehow neither of us went through any dark tunnels, as most describe their exits.

How lucky can a soul be, to share such an experience with an enlightened one who can help us in understanding our Source of Life, Love, and Enlightenment! How often would three different generations of individuals encounter a Near Death Experience (N.D.E.), as the scientific researchers today refer to these similar "traumas"? Now past the age of 85, I know of no others. Neither I, nor my father or grandfather made our stories public.

Each of us played active roles in using our psychic guidance systems to serve others as unobtrusively as possible.

Finding a friend like Gladys Davis was a refresher course in experiencing that Ethereal Light. Through service to all the seekers of Truth who were brought into her sphere, she exuded the vibrations of her soul as an icon of Truth. The characteristic of light calls no attention to itself. Its function is to focus attention on everything else. That is exactly the role Gladys lived, spotlighting accomplishments of individuals and especially her team of co-workers. Pragmatic support, innately applied, was her mantra. As God's Ambassador, her personal contact empowered others to brighten Life around our planet and the space that links our universe with Heaven.

Gladys' name appears most often in association with the works and wonders of Edgar Cayce as his secretary, but she was so much more. For those barely acquainted with his impact on our modern day approach to Life's meaning and purposes, there is a fantastic reservoir of documented records from each phase of his life, archived for perusal by all who wish to observe. Had she not saved them, his contribution to the world would have been limited to the knowledge of a few thousand individuals, rather than the billions who can be enlightened through their study, now technologically available to all A.R.E. members around the world.

PART THREE

Gladys focused on making the Edgar Cayce Readings useful and available to the world beyond the individuals who initially requested the seer's help. Physicians, pharmacists, students of holistic medicine, scholars, loyal members of the A.R.E. and future seekers could also benefit from the Readings, whose access could be found nowhere else. Gladys, as guardian of the preservation of the Readings, undertook the task of organizing and indexing their content for future research and study.

When the Readings for an individual described natural and herbal remedies for treatment, pharmacists were challenged by the attending physicians to locate some of the strange plants, barks, leaves, roots and oils prescribed. This was at a time in our history when medicine was dependent on "herbologists" such as my great-grandmother, a forerunner of female physicians back when the first U.S. college of medicine was in Charleston, South Carolina. During the Civil War, the responsibility to tend the sick fell to the women when all the male doctors left to join the troops. My grandmother, a teenager at the time, was enlisted to ride with her mother in a horse-drawn buggy as her assistant. Knowledge was mainly passed from person to person and there was little standardization in the process of making medicines.

No records from the individual pharmacists of their recipes and methods of preparation had been collected during the early phase of Mr. Cayce's Readings. When Tom Johnson was inspired to package the ingredients recommended for ailments prescribed in the Readings, he discovered Gladys had already been busy, indexing references of similarities in symptoms and ingredients for future medical analysis. This was at a time when all compilations were made by hand, a daunting task in light of today's technology, but one which personified Gladys' dedication to the work. She proved once again to be, as noted below, "invaluable."

In our search for memory contributions from long-time friends of Gladys, I sent word to Tom through a mutual friend, Carol Baraff, who had been his "Right Hand" assistant through many years. Carol is the niece of Al Turner, Gladys' first husband, and mother of one of my granddaughter Alexis' best friends, Jessica. She and her husband, Jim, have been among the young superstars of A.R.E. since its heyday of the sixties and seventies. Carol graciously donated to me two books that her cousin, Doris Patterson, wrote about their uncle: *"The Light In The Mirror,"* and *"The Man With Nine Lives."* Then she also sent me Tom Johnson's letter. He is a very busy man, whose compassion I have witnessed through the years helping many mutual friends. As usual, Gladys had known from their first contact that "Tom was sent for a special job with the Work." He shares recall of her role in his life:

> In the early 1970s when the Heritage Store was still just getting started, Gladys Davis was extremely helpful and encouraging to me. Researching what Edgar Cayce had to say about various formulas, and often how to make them, was extremely time-consuming, and Gladys always gave my questions her full attention. She provided numerous helpful suggestions (and corrections) and even directed me to a local lab that made formulas for me for years. I know she cared a great deal about following Cayce's instructions to the letter, and did her best to make sure I was doing so.
>
> I was especially impressed when our competitor at the time suddenly lost their source of supply for the formulas and Gladys suggested that the owner use us. For several years afterwards, we made the products for that company.

> Tom Johnson, Owner
> The Heritage Store

Virginia Beach native, Bill Jennings, who, at 96 years young today still resides at the beach, recalls the period. At the time, he was a chemist qualified by the Federal Drug Administration (FDA) who was sought by Tom Johnson to produce the formulas to be sold to the public as "Non-prescription Drugs." Excerpts of his story follows:

In 1968 Mr. Tom Johnson, who later founded The Heritage Store in Virginia Beach, called me for an appointment and brought in some samples of what was supposed to be the same product described in one of Edgar Cayce's Readings. On examination of these two samples they were different in appearance and odor. Mr. Johnson told me that he was very interested in the A.R.E. (Association for Research and Enlightenment) but he thought that someone with the proper background and facilities should be making the products for distribution to the A.R.E. members. He had checked me out and he wanted to persuade me to take on this project. I declined at first as I had plenty of work to keep me busy. He then showed me several copies of Edgar Cayce's Readings where he had recommended various mixtures of natural products to treat several different types of illnesses. I asked him to leave these Readings with me for a couple of days and I would call him. I took the Readings home with me and studied them. Then I called a friend who worked at the A.R.E. and asked what the A.R.E. thought of the idea. Her reply was "Thank God for someone interested in doing this. I have run into the same problems that Tom Johnson did and a reliable central source of these products sounds fabulous." I called Tom and set up a meeting for lunch where we wouldn't be disturbed and consented to give it a try on a small scale on formulas that were used topically and not taken internally.

My friend at A.R.E. introduced me to Gladys Davis who was Edgar Cayce's secretary and who was present when all of the Readings took place. She thought the idea of having one reliable source of the Cayce products filled a big void. We became good friends and she furnished me all the Readings I needed to compile a formula list of the various products.

For a while, Gladys and I would meet for lunch once a week, and she would furnish a new batch of Mr. Cayce's formulas, which I studied and had a physician check out. Since many of the cases had multiple disorders and he had not spelled out the specifics for each cause, the research was tedious. Gladys' follow-up with the families of each participant was invaluable. She was an exceptionally intelligent woman, and one of the finest people that I have ever known.

To create the products in my laboratory required a special license to do so. The next time the FDA brought me samples for analysis I explained to them what I was doing with the A.R.E. products and asked him if he thought I could get an FDA Pharmaceutical Manufacturing License. He replied that he doubted if I could, as the FDA didn't have a high regard for herbal medicines, but he would take it up with the Drug Division and let me know. Surprisingly, a few days later I received a call from the Drug Division of FDA and was told that they would issue me a manufacturing license subject to their inspection. He also told me that although the FDA didn't approve of herbal medicine, they concluded that due to the complexity of many of the Cayce formulae, the difficulty obtaining some of the raw materials and the questionable purity of these items they felt that a supervised source of compounding these formulae would be protection against harm coming to the users of these formulae.

A couple of days later they sent an inspector to my laboratory. He made several suggestions which I agreed to and I would receive my license as a "Non-prescription Drug Custom Manufacturer." As soon as I made one batch of each product and furnished the FDA with samples of each product along with a sample of each ingredient used and a copy of each formula. The FDA picked up the samples and about a month later I received my official license.

I made a total of 31 different Cayce formulae. As time passed herbal medicine became popular and other people made similar products, so I felt it was time to get out of the pharmaceutical business as my chemical laboratory had expanded and I needed to spend more time there. I made the Cayce formulae for several years.

I am certainly glad that Tom Johnson introduced me to the Cayce products. While I was skeptical at first about Edgar Cayce and his teachings, I soon gained the highest esteem for him. Cayce found that in almost every case nature provides a cure for every illness. I also believe that over the past twenty years or so we have made great strides in finding the nature of, and the source for these cures.

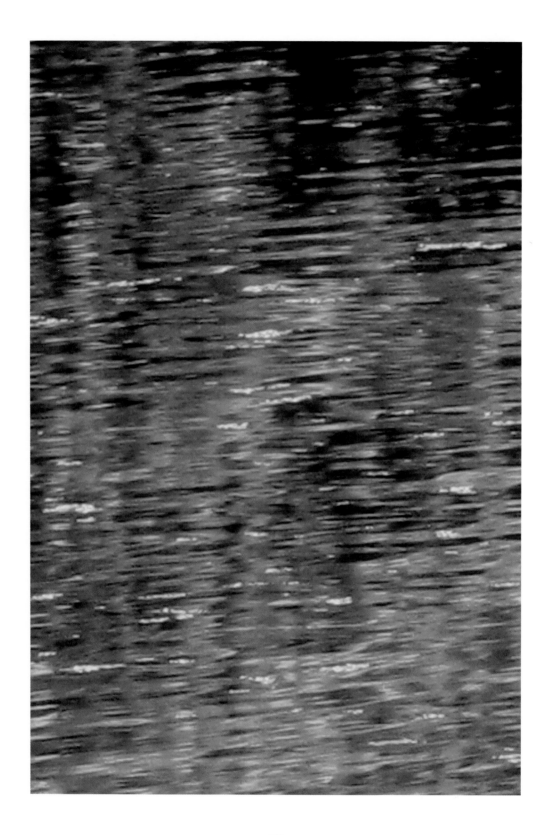

Recycling Our Tribe

My next-door neighbor, in years gone by, was the answer to a long-time fervent prayer. At the time I needed a special kind of friend, so I pestered God with persistent pleas. Finally, I think He tired of my begging and sent a special envoy from His service department of experts to silence my whining. I recognized her on sight the day Margaret Shaw Brent moved in. Our relationship developed into a friendship that endured until God retrieved her from this plane many years ago.

We shared our interests and concerns with family and friends. Introduced to Edgar Cayce through her son's connections, both of us became involved in his field of Work. Our backgrounds of Bible study and church activities, coupled with an interest in comparative religions' identity of One Source of Life's Eternal Force, bonded our sisterhood. Her son, James Ethan Brent, befriended me through the ensuing years, as we have continued the joy of sharing our mutual interest and friendships from that period of our lives.

Margaret Brent

If Ethan had not brought to my doorstep the Edgar Cayce legacy, Gladys and I may have missed our connections during this lifetime. It was he who first introduced us to *"There Is A River,"* by Thomas Sugrue, which led to Edgar Cayce, the A.R.E., and ultimately to Gladys Davis. As a mutual friend of Gladys, he has helped me in the early days of editing and preparing this manuscript for print. He expressed his own recollection, and shared his mother's picture and the note Gladys wrote her. I have included it as a sample of their close friendship and the way Gladys added so many items of pertinent value to the archives of A.R.E. Applying her marvelous memory and organizational skills to the requests of others seeking information for their articles, books and research, she made Edgar Cayce's contribution more valid to science and academia than would have otherwise been possible. It was her far-reaching vision of the future which allowed this to happen, a dedication which surpassed the already daunting "job" of recording the Readings. No one was closer to the organizational side of the Work than she.

Margaret's charisma and spiritual attunement was a magnet that drew admirers from every avenue of life. She and Gladys, both Aquarians, beautiful and of kindred natures, doubled my benefits through their friendships as the decades passed. The humility they both exuded in their innocence of worldliness amazed me as they served their less refined brothers and sisters. Seemingly unaware of their superior qualities, neither sought to step in line ahead of others in the maze of human endeavors. As keen observers of the stars on stage, both served as boosters of others while avoiding spotlights on themselves. Always encouraging with support and approval, their service reflected their closely-held ideals of feminine virtue and modesty.

Our acquaintance with pioneers of A.R.E. was shared with mutual appreciation, as our interests in Unity had been. Eula and Harold Allen, among those early associates of Edgar Cayce, were mentors for us as we joined the ranks of membership in prayer and study groups. Harold was an editor of A.R.E.'s early literary promotions after retiring as a Naval officer. His Reading by Edgar Cayce described his past life as an advisor of the Egyptian Pharoah during the Ra-Ta period. Pharoah was a previous incarnation of Hugh Lynn Cayce, Edgar's oldest son. Edgar Cayce had lived during the period as the priest, Ra-Ta, who, with Gertrude, who had lived as Isis, had been forced into exile by the Pharoah, leaving behind their infant daughter as hostage. Gladys, identified as "Iso," the infant daughter of Ra-Ta, was cared for by Harold and his wife and others in that incarnation. Their efforts to bring the parents back home eventually succeeded, but, not until that "perfect child," Iso, had died.

Eula's Reading had identified her as active in the Temple of Sacrifice in Egypt, helping rid humans of their animal appendages and obtain pure bodies. Edgar Cayce indicated her awareness of Biblical Genesis which became evident

as she taught in lectures, provided individual education and authored a trilogy of books: *"Before the Beginning," "The River of Time,"* and *"You are Forever."*

I felt extremely fortunate to have been among their close friends, as were the Brents, who nurtured both of them through their final years. As mutual friends of Gladys and the Cayce family, the "old Hippy" (as Eula tagged herself through the sixties and seventies, while shepherding the youths swarming to the Beach) was as interesting a character as any one could know. (Eula #2454, Harold #2746). Their son was identified as the "rich young ruler" that Jesus encountered. In the Bible version, when told to give away his riches, in order to join Him, he turned away. Edgar Cayce's Reading stated that he returned home, gave away everything, then ultimately came back and joined the disciples.

So many of the Readings provided us with more detailed accounts of events that were just "sound bites" in the Biblical references. I heartily recommend their study as parallel reading and as aids in understanding your possible connections to the individuals and events of scriptural history. An old hymn comes to mind, *"Were You There When They Crucified My Lord?"* Details from his Readings may verify your own recall. Former incarnations of anyone may be recalled, with their own keys to soul memories, as Cayce often stated.

A note from Gladys to Margaret follows. Gladys never missed an opportunity to express her "Gladitude" to fellow helpful souls.

April 10, 1978

Dearest Margaret:-

Thanks so much for that precious picture of Eula in her garden at 1190 Harmony Road, Norfolk, in 1973. I am putting it in the A.R.E. archival box of pictures for that year. It is perhaps the best late one we have on file.

The beautiful, rare book you gave me at Eula's memorial service at her home in Mathews on March 2, 1978, which belonged to your grandfather, W.S. Shaw - THE HEALING OF THE NATIONS by Charles Linton - has been turned over to the A.R.E. Reference Library for safe keeping and for reference only. Charlotte Schoen, Librarian, was very enthusiastic about it, as we did not have a copy - although the subject matter- coming from the psychic realms - was touched on in several other publications during that time period. It was the beginning of psychic research in this country. Thanks so much. It will be invaluable in the overall picture.

Bless you and yours.

Love,

Gladys

Organizing

Adding pertinent librarian material to the archives was Gladys' constant obsession in documenting the trail of Edgar Cayce for future students of the Work. Protecting the personal identity of the "number-coded individuals" whose Readings could provide counsel on successful achievements, or dismal failures that tested them, was a responsibility that Gladys kept sacred. Often she was asked to participate as a speaker by sharing her views on the Work. She preferred participation as a panel member in presenting anecdotes of Edgar Cayce as a seer, and as an ordinary person of normal, down-to-earth qualities. But, occasionally, she would agree to stand alone at the podium to share her recollections of him and the individuals that contributed to the early support groups. She wrote articles for publications or lectures, when necessary, on pertinent aspects of the Readings. On one such occasion, she was talking about the prayer group members, and shared a story about Edith Edmonds. As I heard Gladys say her name, I said, "That's Martha, the sister of Mary and Lazarus," to a friend beside me. Embarrassed that my thoughts being whispered had distracted Gladys, who managed to move on through her lecture, I wanted to hide my blushing face.

On our way home Gladys asked, "Did I inadvertently let a cat out of the bag?" I replied, "No, Gladys, you didn't say anything but her name. I've heard her name in the line-up of that group many times before, but when you said 'Edith' I realized her Bethany linkage. Gladys, I am truly sorry that it tumbled out of my mouth. I had no intention of doing that." She laughed, patted me on my shoulder, okaying my blunder. She understood my untamed psyche.

"Sometimes, I can't help it," I said. "My tongue has a loose bolt on its clamp. When the brain rattles, it blurts. Thank Goodness, it sleeps through most lectures."

"Your tongue sleeps?" she asked.

"Never, Honey. Just my brain." I loved to hear her laugh. Being a clown for Gladys was the best job I ever had. Les Wilmore, who became Gladys' second husband, knew its rewards, too, as did her friends who tickled her with antics and funny stories.

Tribe Members

Mary Ann Woodward and I experienced some past life memory-jolting events from our close association with Mildred Davis, Shane Miller, Ruth Burks and Irene Harrison. We recalled past lives in ancient Caesarea where Jesus visited His sister, Ruth, her husband, Philoas, and their children. Some lifetimes seem more potent than others in triggering recall. Mr. Cayce found it easier to recognize others from lifetimes where he had strong relationships as well. For your further study, I highly recommend this group's Readings as each one has given me permission to identify them. Their numbers are: Mary Ann, #2487, Mildred Davis, #295, Ruth Burks, #3175 and the Harrisons, #1158 and #1151.

When Mr. Burkhalter, Ruth Burks' first husband, was hospitalized, a Health Reading was requested of Mr. Cayce. Realizing that the patient was formerly Nicodemus, he invited Ruth to visit Virginia Beach when she finished the legal settlements of his estate. Seeing that help was too late to save her husband's life, he wished to renew her friendship, as he had known her during that New Testament incarnation, and enlist her healing aid. She did come, and he gave a Life Reading for her that she, as the wife of Nicodemus in that lifetime, had made the exquisite pearl grey robe for Jesus, for

Ruth Burks and Mildred Davis

which the soldiers drew lots to own as He hung on the cross. She was asked by Mr. Cayce, because of her psychic healing ability, to tune in with him during some of his Readings for the most seriously ill patients. She agreed to comply, so thereafter Gladys called her in advance of such scheduled appointments. She was linked to the Healing Group (#281) and tuned in during their sessions. Such recognitions were not always made during Readings, but often occurred during his conscious state when he met otherwise "passing strangers."

Many of us experience the vibrational signals even as we draw blanks of names, dates and details from associations in past lifetimes. The connection of our conscious memory may be less proficient than Mr. Cayce's ability to retain awareness in an unbroken chain of diverse linkage. Each of us can improve on our soul's potential to utilize those gifts. Jesus ventured to promise such enlightenment. Some take advantage of that assistance.

Ruth Burks and Micki Kluge

Irene Harrison with Micki and her granddaughters Alexis and Jesse

Ruth Burks (#3175) was among the most astute psychics of that nature that I knew, whose clairvoyance enhanced her healing assistance to Arthur, her second husband. As he traveled the globe, writing for *Life Magazine*, accompanied by their expert staff photographers, his exploits were recorded and shared with the world. Visiting some of its most remote areas, his participation with Shamans of exotic tribal vintage as healers, Ruth attuned her spiritual connections as each patient was being treated. As editor, and founder of the first American publication of a periodical of paranormal articles, *"Mind Digest,"* she applied her exceptional intellect. Mr. Cayce's request for her participation during the crucial Health Readings often united the support of local prayer group members.

Arthur Burks was a close friend of Tom Sugrue, Manly P. Hall, Shane Miller, Walter and Lao Russell, all fascinating scholars of the Bible and philosophical aspects of life during the period of Edgar Cayce's tenure. Memory fails me as to which comic strip artist was the one of their friends to whom they fed ideas, whether it was Alex Raymond, (*Flash Gordon*, I believe) or Phil Nowlan (*Buck Rogers*) as a part of their group. Since they shared ideas and writing, art and Cayce concepts, I could not resist sharing this sideline distraction. *Mea culpa!*

During this period my family life was more conducive to greater involvement with the fieldwork of A.R.E. as I took on the coordination of Search For God (S.F.G.) study group work with members in the Richmond area, as growing numbers of people became interested in joining us. My trips to the Virginia Beach headquarters increased so that Gladys and I shared more social time together. In January and February, especially, since there were less active lecture programs on the agenda, Gladys took her vacation time during the winter months. Her visits in my home were easier for her to plan, and I thoroughly enjoyed celebrating with a birthday party that allowed the Richmond groups to share her presence. Like a happy child, she made those occasions such a treat for all of us.

In September of 1973, I prepared, iced and decorated "Cream Cheese Pound Cake," loaded my car and hauled it to the Cavalier Hotel in Virginia Beach which I had reserved for a Golden Anniversary celebrating Gladys' fifty years with the Work. During the six months prior, I had badgered Hugh

Lynn to plan the event so that members throughout America might arrange to attend. For reasons I did not understand, he did not feel the event was conducive with A.R.E.'s programming. Being self-determined, I decided to go it alone, although I had no means of delivering the invitations except through personal contact and faith. In August, Hugh Lynn was invited to attend the Open House at the Cavalier from noon to 6:00 P.M.

Only then did he allow plans to add a dinner party with speakers to make the celebration of her fifty years with the Work official.

Gladys was as adorable as any child can be at a birthday party. "In all my life, I've never seen that much cake, or one more beautiful to me," she exclaimed to me. What more delightful appraisal could a pastry chef hope for? Decorated layers on huge platters were transported to be served along the entire beachfront to Virginia Beach's tourists by a crew of happy celebrants of Gladys' fan club.

Stuffed with cake, punch, nuts and mints, the guests ate dinner with Gladys as A.R.E.'s speakers shared Gladitude. It is an event that epitomizes the desires of any child who dreams of an ideal meal with thousands of slices of cake served as the appetizer.

Gladys celebrating her 50th anniversary with the Work, 1973.

A Half Century Tribute Is Paid For Dedication

By Helen Crist, Beacon Correspondent

Virginia Beach—Even one not attuned to psychic phenomena would have felt the good vibrations recently at the Cavalier Hotel...and understandably so, since it was a reception and testimonial dinner for Gladys Davis Turner.

The celebration marked the 50th year that Gladys has dedicated herself to the readings of the late psychic, Edgar Cayce, and to the Association for Research and Enlightenment, Inc.

For 20 of those years, she was Cayce's secretary. And for 11 years, she undertook the task, along with her staff, of filing some 14,249 readings under more than 200,000 subject headings.

Her friends came from far and near to honor her. One, Mrs. William R. Kluge, of Richmond, brought along a four-tier cake that she baked especially for the occasion.

There were accolades at the testimonial dinner from Hugh Lynn Cayce, A.R.E. president; and from Mrs. Helen Ellington and Mrs. Ruth Lenoir, charter members of the first Study Group.

Throughout the afternoon reception, Gladys, tall and erect, wearing blue, an orchid corsage at her shoulder, a few purple wild flowers at her wrist, moved quickly among her friends, speaking rapidly as she does, putting all at ease.

And for us, several days later, there was a two-hour conversation in her small office at A.R.E. headquarters.

"It's a little cramped in here," she said with a laugh, as she stood on a stool and searched for a particular item.

A glance about the room, particularly at the wall, was a key to her personality. Every available space, it seemed, was covered with favorite mementos—letters, post cards, pictures of the Cayce family with whom she lived, of her own family, gifts, souvenirs. Flowers brightened the windows.

She was only 18, when she became Edgar Cayce's secretary—and then only by chance...or was it?

Gladys said she knew of Cayce in her hometown of Selma, Ala., as a good photographer and a fine Sunday School teacher at First Christian Church.

At the time she was employed at Tissier's Hardware Store. A friend there asked her one day if she would do her a favor and record a reading that Cayce was to give for her nephew, who was seriously ill.

Unknown to Gladys, Cayce was at that time advertising for a stenographer. Up until then, when readings were given, the persons obtaining them brought their own stenographers, or they were simply taken down in choppy longhand, Gladys said.

So she agreed to help her friend.

She went to the Cayce Art Company, where the reading would be held. There were maybe 10 people in the room, she said. There was a couch there. Edgar's father conducted the reading.

"Mr. Cayce came in and talked to us for a few minutes explaining what he would do. His shirt sleeves were rolled up—it was a hot summer day—and then he lay down on his back on the sofa.

He put his hands over the solar plexus, took a series of deep short breaths, gazed at the ceiling, and his eyelids began to flutter."

It was at that point, Gladys said, that his father gave him the name and address of the person for whom the reading was requested. Cayce repeated this slowly, describing the blood supply, the nervous system and organs of the subject. Then he recommended treatment.

Of course, the clairvoyant could only do this in a state of self-hypnosis; awake, he knew nothing of medicine.

"Were you frightened or awed by it?" we asked.

"No, not at all. You see, Mr. Cayce had such personal magnetism. It wasn't that he consciously did anything to attract a person. He was so human, so natural and so at ease, that I simply thought that maybe a lot of people could do this thing."

And because she was merely helping a friend out by recording the reading, she

was all the more astounded when, as a result of her proficiency, she was offered a permanent position with the Cayce family. She felt so right about it, that she wasted no time at all accepting.

Gladys said that very few people in Selma were aware of Cayce's psychic ability.

Coincidentally, that's the way it was when she came with the family in 1925 to Virginia Beach to live.

It was during a reading that the psychic selected the Beach for permanent quarters, declaring it ideal for "the work" because of the healing qualities of the ocean and the sand.

We wondered why there was a tendency to conceal the readings.

"Well, it's just that people didn't understand what we were doing, and you know when people don't grasp what you're talking about, it gets easier not to mention it," Gladys said.

In fact, one of her friends on 35th St., where they first lived, asked her what Mr. Cayce's business was. Laughing, she said, "I told them he was a writer—I simply didn't know how to explain it."

This tendency to concealment may not be a good thing today, she said. "Lots of people think we're doing crazy things, when if they really knew what we were doing, they might not be so critical."

At any rate, Gladys fell in love with the Beach. The daily walks to pick up the mail from the one-room post office where the parking lot is now, behind Barr's Pharmacy on 17th Street at Atlantic Ave., were a real treat. She'd walk along a dirt path by the trolley tracks. That path is now Pacific Avenue.

Many books have been written detailing the events of the Cayce family, of which Gladys remained a vital part.

"Is the A.R.E. accepted, after all these years, by the Beach people?" we asked.

"Oh, I think so. After all, it's known world-wide. It's been written up in magazines, books... we have ministers, psychiatrists, doctors, parapsychologists studying here."

(Continued on page 15)

Gladys really enjoyed sharing food and fun with others. Michael Reidy remembered that one day while working with her, she invited him to join her for lunch at her house. Her great nephew, Michael, (son of Eva and T.J.) was to be a special guest for hot dogs, the way he liked her to cook them. In her role of acting as any grandmother would attempt, she created a child's Southern dream. Sauteing the frankfurters in bacon grease, rolling them in maple syrup before wrapping in warm bun blankets, she served them with condiments of mustard, pickles, chopped onions, cole slaw and potato salad. Reidy remembered them as the best hot dogs he had ever tasted as they shared their happy time with little Michael and his beloved "Granny."

Testimonial Reception Honors Cayce Friend

(Continued from page 14)

But she adds a note of caution.

"It seems like there are psychics popping up all over the place, here and everywhere. But the way they use their ability is sometimes questionable."

She said that many who came to conferences at ARE in the past, would give readings on the side for money. On this, she would like to set the record straight.

"We do not approve of this. We don't recommend any psychic, or sponsor any, nor do we set ourselves up as an authority on the subject."

We asked if she expected to see Edgar Cayce again.

"Oh yes," she said smiling. "I feel that all souls are working together through eons of time. I feel that many of us have been closely associated with him in previous life experiences. I fully expect to work with him again."

"Do you fear death?"

"No—I believe in immortality. Although I believe it's possible to communicate with those who have passed through God's door, I know that Mr. Cayce didn't advise us to try to do this. He said it was unwise to look to a departed entity for advice."

"Do you expect to come back to earth?"

"Oh yes, I hope so—I like it here."

New Age Wonders

The twentieth century had begun as the "New Age" of Theological expansion in America. With the birth of a number of "new thought" movements such as Mary Baker Eddy's Christian Science and Unity's Center of Leaders (Filmores, Cadys), the influx of influence from abroad such as the Theosophical Society and Rudolph Steiner's Anthroposophy, Eastern studies of ancient religious roots of Buddhism, Hinduism, Islam and even Zoroastrianism added hues of insight for these expansive thinkers. So, when Edgar Cayce's Readings became a part of the mix being discussed by the Orthodox Bible students and teachers, the fertile soil of intellectual curiosity engendered public interest in their phenomenal expressions. Among the intellectual giants whose work I find fascinating was that of Manley P. Hall, with his in-depth studies of other cultures and belief systems. All these religions found reference in Cayce's extensive coverage.

In an excerpt from *"December, 1936, A Monthly Letter,"* Manley P. Hall states:

> There is no great teacher whose doctrines have been more intentionally misunderstood than those of Jesus, but the intelligent thinker is able to distinguish clearly between Christianity and "Churchianity." Churchianity prays and pleads and exhorts with formulas for every failing of the soul, washing out all the sins of man with holy water. The real teaching of Jesus simply states: that he who lives the life shall know the doctrine.

The early church, patterned after pagan Mysteries, sought for a little time to perpetuate the arcana, but such a procedure would doom the church to a humble and obscure existence, ministering only to a devout and dedicated few. The bishops of the church were mortal men instinctively desiring power and authority, and they sacrificed the spiritual doctrines of Christianity to temporal ambitions. The church gained temporal power at the expense of spiritual authority.

As the means of transportation and communication expanded our frontiers, the subjects of miracle cures for those beyond the scope of medical science, as then understood, was electrifying. Curious extensions of mental, physical and spiritual coordinates opened a Pandora's box of mysteries to expose new analytical evaluations. Theories once harnessed by fear of revelation came through the veils of ridicule to be considered weird, although to some people, maybe even reasonable, as explanatory possibilities. Strange coincidences extended avenues of their potential discovery, as a new path in understanding mankind's purpose in Life-and-Death cycles. When a book by Noel Langley included a chapter on *"The Hidden History of Reincarnation,"* I found the plausible answer for which I had searched to understand since birth, the many past-life recalls I had experienced. If his facts could be verified, I surmised, I could accept and trust that my own memories were valid recollections.

On reading Langley's account of the Biblical revisions made during the reign of the Emperor Justinian, when his wife, Empress Theodora, chose to delete all reference to the theory of reincarnation from the Scriptures, I had to investigate further. Living in Richmond, Virginia, at the time, I found easy access to research secular history in the libraries of the University of Richmond Theology Department, Union Theology Seminary and the City Library downtown. I found that their records were available for all seminary scholars, verifying that the egotistical Empress did, indeed, have those Popes murdered who refused to tamper with the sacred texts of Biblical records of the Roman World. When she found her willing survivor to fulfill her destructive edict, his staff worked prodigiously to expunge all reference to the concepts of previous or future earth incarnations. Eager to survive, her victim Pope managed to have deleted to her satisfaction any words that hinted of any reason or reference to karmic debts.

A number of implications, obscure though they may be, were left intact in the Bible, such as in the healing of the blind Bartemaeus. When the disciples failed to restore sight to the man, born blind, they asked Jesus, "Whose sin was responsible, Bartemaeus or his father?" Whose karma is he bearing? How could a fetus sin in the womb? Why would God punish an infant? Such concerns beg for greater understanding. When Jesus explained that in this particular case there was no sin, but that the works of God should be made manifest in him. Willing to live in visual darkness, establishing that challenge for the world to observe so that he could serve a noble purpose in honor of his Master, Jesus, on this public occasion reveals such a deeper measure of life's purpose than the disciples were superficially aware; where, prior to one's lifetime, a soul chooses a state of being to produce a desired outcome or learning experience. Thus, we have a precedent that merits God's Law in that we are not equipped to judge others. The whole ninth chapter of the Gospel according to John refers to this healing and its concerns among the Jews of that era.

In another case, when Jesus asked his disciples who the masses identified Him as having been, they responded with names of past prophets. Elias, or Elijah was often named, but they knew that His cousin, John the Baptist was really the reincarnation of Elijah. Other references have similarly mystified scholars in the past. Some have been among the questions posed to Edgar Cayce, whose answers provide a fascinating study of reincarnation through the Readings he gave.

Theodora succeeded with such thoroughness, however, in discarding most references that, for the intervening centuries, no confident successor dared to refute the alterations. There were probably many other pertinent details of the various scribes lost to the Scriptures from such diabolic episodes throughout the Bible's history. Edgar Cayce, as well as many other scholars and teachers, was able to add so many lost passages of information. Archeologists have dug up corroborating evidence since his death, much as Mr. Cayce foresaw. More is yet to be revealed which will bear out his prophesies.

Ineffable Mystique Opens Search

At three years of age, and not yet having learned to read, my quoting and discussing scriptural excerpts attracted the attention of my elders. Treated as a curiosity in the 1920s, the extrasensory levels of awareness placed a burden of wariness on my relationships. Misunderstanding frustrated me as much as others. Forecasting events with the intent to caution those whom I saw endangered were met with total apprehension. When the event occurred, their usual assumption implied that I had put a "hex" on the individual. It was thought since I accurately predicted an event that I mentally desired the harm that was executed through some demonic power. Shades of witchcraft shadowed my presence, causing me a guilt complex of cruel uncontrollable concerns. Compounding my dilemma was the strange capacity as a channel of healing through touch. Pains and fevers were diminished when my hands were placed on the head of a patient in answer to my silent prayers. Life was definitely confusing until I read Tom Sugrue's book, *"There Is A River,"* and discovered Edgar Cayce. My empathy for him was profound. To learn how he had been able to use his psychic abilities for helping others freed me of the "witchcraft" guilt plague.

When I was reunited with the Pioneers of A.R.E., I found assembled a menagerie of souls who were also attracted to share the mission of Edgar Cayce and his twin soul, Gladys Davis. My own concepts found verification among them. There were references to places such as Temples of Sacrifice, or of Enlightenment, increasing appreciation of Arts and Beauty from Atlantis, through Egypt, Persia, Judea, Rome, France, Early America and today. Is it any wonder that many have been able to recognize each other from past encounters?

Gladys' favorite past lifetime was Persian, as, Ilya, the wife of Uhjltd, indicated in the Readings as Edgar Cayce. Their son was Zend, an earlier lifetime of Jesus. Gladys chose to remain "on the other side" when He returned as Jesus, the son of His own twin soul, Mary. Gladys' role as a devoted guardian angel, according to her Reading, was vital in behalf of His mission and also for Mr. Cayce, as Lucius. Practice in the role of such guardianship is high among her specialties. For her nephew, who had been Alexander the Great, she had played a supervisory role in helping him prepare for each step of his escapades in bridging communication with his contacts. She remains active in her role as overseer of her legacy in the Work as many experience her promptings even now.

Since her transition in 1986, I am aware of Gladys' helpful role for a number of individuals, myself included. A couple of miraculous healings occurred as she appeared to the recipients. "The Work," as she had often referred to A.R.E.'s role, has continued to be of concern to her, as it must also be for Edgar Cayce and his family. His wife, Gertrude, was the twin soul of Hugh Lynn, their son. Mrs. Cayce also remained on the other side as a guardian for Hugh Lynn during his life as Andrew, Jesus' first chosen Disciple. Of those "pioneers" of the Search For God and Healing Groups, I have often seen their continued participation since they left this plane.

Being reunited at A.R.E. with souls of the Judean period of Jesus' lifetime has been the most challenging to put into perspective for me. It is also the most stimulating to my overall sense of purpose. Even as a child, I recognized many individuals that shared that special era. Usually our relationships were easy to appreciate from initial contacts. Mutual fondness was immediate, though our former identities were not always specific or sorted out. Family members' roles, being so close with present life inter-action, blurred the process of recall from former associations. Acceptance came without the sense of unfamiliarity that new acquaintances seem to trigger. We don't differentiate the vibrations in the same way as when our systems are alerted by new faces. No alarms go off. It's more like wearing old shoes that have conformed to the feet so well that our awareness takes them for granted. Comfort allows freedom for other concerns.

Painful relations may trigger the memory so as to adapt the dream mechanisms or other aids in unraveling mysteries of the soul. Aura contacts are like that for me, at least, not by pain, but sensing the energy stimulation. However, there are occasions of long-standing friendships that, under some changes in circumstances, mood or event, can open the line of communi-cation between souls, bringing revelations of recognition that had eluded detection of former relationships.

Mary Ann Woodward and I had known each other for years before we suddenly realized, in 1968, the whole panorama of our close association in Judea. As I studied the Readings, I became fascinated in the realization that so many souls had chosen to incarnate together in groups throughout the ages, particularly those advanced souls surrounding the time of Jesus. The Readings supported our personal soul memories and allowed us new freedom in following their threads. We began an intense phase of co-ordinating a team of our old buddies to write about the events of our roles as we experienced them during Jesus' lifetime. We identified our group as *"Dinosaurs, Not Yet Quite Extinct."* Our sessions together produced a lot of shared memories with details that have never before been printed, though the book was begun. Each of us agreed to allow our total identities to be publicized. Each had a personal relationship with Jesus, some closer than others.

Scattered across the globe, our reunions suffered the fates of separation by time and space, and the epistles expanded and contracted with uncanny events. We managed to stay in communication with each other until, one by one, each left this plane. As the last survivor, I do not think that composite manuscript will be published, but the exercise was stimulating, and some of the encounters are shared herein.

In the meantime, it's interesting to sort through renditions of other writers' versions, surmising about that period of history. Occasionally segments of their stories ring true enough to open the windows of long hidden clues from within self. More often there is a glaring evidence of Theodora's mischief in altering the premise of circumstances. The theory of reincarnation is one of controversy for the Western World, though the ice has been broken for open minds to allow for its consideration. Great strides have been made in the communication field as science and religions are approaching more common ground. However, frauds also can mesmerize us.

Technology advancements such as carbon dating and archeological discoveries play an interesting role in the verification of information such as that given in the Readings through Edgar Cayce. In the mid-sixties, I dreamed about the coins placed on the eyes of Jesus in the tomb after His physical death on the cross. As I recorded the dream, I drew a sketch of the coins, noting that they were Pontius Pilate's effort to honor Caesar Tiberius and legally usable for only two years. A couple of days later, during a visit with friends, I saw a ceramic dish embellished with the same designs, so I shared the dream and the sketch. "Some day, these coin images on the Shroud of Turin will verify it by their date, leaving no doubt of its authenticity." Through all the tests of challenging studies, for me there was no doubt because of that lucid dream.

Science has erased the uncertainty for others as well. After years of many different approaches to challenges in proving its validity, a woman saw that the sample patch used for carbon dating had been of a different weave from the original linen cloth. Proving that it was a cotton thread patch that was more easily dyed to match the ancient linen at the time of its needed repair, the scientists who had saved scraps from their original allotments for testing willingly gave up their linen scraps for more carbon dating. Proof at last that left no room for doubt that the unique relic of Jesus' shroud has survived history as an indelible photographic record of His Crucifixion; and when all the mystery about its visible image is understood, it may verify the event of His Resurrection as well.

My evaluations of human history may be freckled with flaws, riddled with gaping distortions and inordinate ignorance. Nevertheless, our recorded history has gaps where so few scholars can fill in the details for us, so I am particularly grateful to have access to these Readings. Linked through thousands of individual lives, Edgar Cayce brought forth details explaining how, as many of those entities were previously involved, they returned to carry on roles of being humanity's spiritual leaders.

Edgar Cayce's role during the Persian period is among my favorites of his shared experiences. The Readings locate him in that lifetime as the parent of Zend, who became the founder of Zoroastrianism which is still one of India's and Iran's major religions. The Readings detail a fascinating story of the culture at the crossroads of an exotic period of history when caravans of camels laden with silks, spices, jewels, grains and herbal concoctions dared tempt the fates of survival. Tribal competitions previewed the challenges still apparent in today's politically volatile world.

The incarnations of the soul entity who eventually evolved as Jesus, or Emanuel (God with us), according to Cayce's Readings, began as Adam in the Hebrew record of the Torah, or our Old Testament. In references of other ancient religions, there are links to various leaders who were listed as precedents of Jesus such as the Buddha of India, Zend, Adam, Enoch, Melchizedek, as Abraham's guide and author of the Book of Job, Asaph, the Psalmist, Joseph and Joshua. Scattered throughout the Readings, mention of individual links to one or more of these entities refer to each as the "first begotten Son of God," as being the same soul-entity. Among my preferences of A.R.E. books that cover this is *"Lives of the Master,"* written by Glenn Sandefur, among friends whom I adore.

My Synopsis of Adam's Tour

Although He willingly volunteered in our behalf to lead via example, Adam and His counterpart, Eve, found living in the garden by God's rules too great a challenge. Then, as Enoch, He walked so well-balanced on God's path that He escaped Death when vacating Earth's premises. Later, Noah's life was a lesson in obedience to God's direct instructions to save some remnants of Adam's covenant for a cleaned-up new start.

Abraham's role in repopulation of heirs to the spiritual kingdom and the Earth's human options in learning patience and fortitude managed to initiate three major factions of religious contention: Judaism, Christianity and Islam. Even now, the challenges of finding the bond of brotherhood between all of his descendants threatens our mutual survival. God's covenant with Abraham held in replenishing the Earth with many nations, although the karmic debt through brutal emotional relationships has increased accordingly.

Roles of power, control, greed and jealousies have entangled resentments through disagreements of cultural beliefs, even in the methods, creeds and many forms of worship expressing our adoration and gratitude to the Source of our living breath.

The Prophets of Old forewarned Earth's inhabitants and schools of their followers who continue to recycle their messages. Joseph exemplified royally the ideal son and brother, *sans resentment*, while generously displaying kindness and responsible intuitive insight as a leader. Moses, in gathering kindred souls for journeying into the Promised Land, realized their attention deficits and short concentration spans. He requested from God and received a list for Life's guidelines written down on stone tablets. Thanks to those who recited their phrases, their essence has survived for a few scholars to translate them through the centuries as the Golden Rule.

Later, at least, Joshua persevered faithfully as he kept pushing forward toward his goal. I was especially impressed with his example while in control of the ditch diggers during their extended drought in the desert. When all hope of water provision seemed nil, he kept the faith in God as sole provider, insisting that they keep digging ditches to receive the rain although there were no clouds in the sky. Allowing no doubt to interfere, he set the standard of belief at the miraculous level so that when the rains filled the finished vessels, all the people and animals could express their appreciation to the Source of All Supply.

So often, in my lifetime, that example of his Faith-use has been my saving grace. Thus far, I have never seen it fail. But then, my own Dad had underscored its truth during the "Great Depression" as he reminded all of us that "The Lord Provides" followed by his thanksgiving prayers. Thus, we were spared the agonies of want, while feeding all who found the path to our farmhouse. At times, there were many near starvation. I, too, have been spared fear of lack, or need, during this life.

Digging Ditches

Trusting pays dividends, as Joshua's experience proved. I have witnessed often, especially in caring for patients and family, that each of us have faced situations which challenge the budget to meet opportunities which open expanded options. My daughter, Karen's, college roommate had an older sister living in Italy. When her sister invited Emily to spend the summer with her family, she asked her to bring a friend to share the visit. Karen was invited, but the added expenses seemed out of reach for us. Since Emily and Karen were art students attuned to that of the classic masters of Italy's heyday, the opportunity to tour Rome, Florence and the galleries of Europe with a linguist as their chaperone was a phenomenal offer.

Naturally, their desire to go there was a dream both shared with equal enthusiasm, and I felt that such a golden opportunity could hardly be repeated in the years ahead of them. As they discussed ways of fulfilling the dream excursion, I suggested an exercise of applying the faith of Joshua. "Let's dig the ditches to be ready for God's shower."

Karen presented her proposal to her father. Knowing that we had saved for her college education and her next years tuition was safely in the bank, she asked if she might borrow travel funds to take advantage of the "chance of a lifetime." On her return, she would get a job for the year, then return to finish college when her earnings accrued. Her father, having used the GI Bill to get his engineering degree, was by nature much too cautious to trust the fates that a female could earn enough to pay her way. Having been in Europe as a soldier, he was reluctant to allow his only daughter to wander around over there among the "wolves" too far from his protective parental power. Though his anxiety was not vocalized, I understood his masculine opposition to letting his daughter out of reach. Fear paralyzes dreams if allowed permission to exist. Women would never have a child if faith were not innate within their gender. I think that's why God chose to let them have total access to the unique job, since it can't be done without total faith in Life.

With a couple of months to plan, pray, meditate, shop, get immune injections for passport requirements, photos and reservations for flight schedules, we girls did the preliminary preparations for the European excursion, as if it were meant to be God's Will.

College exams were completed for the year. Emily was to leave Virginia on Monday to return to her home in Boston for a few days before heading for Turin, Italy, to join her sister's family. Her last weekend was to be in our home, so, I picked up both of them as we hauled Karen's belongings from their dorm. We forwarded Emily's trunks by freight to Boston and were back home preparing dinner when my husband returned from work Friday evening.

As he joined us in the kitchen he handed me a check. As I studied it, he spoke to Karen and Emily. "I am sorry that I had no idea of this check I received today. Had I known to expect it, you could have made the trip together. I know it's too late to get your passport, Karen, and flight tickets, and..." The whoops of joy erupting from the two girls as they hugged and jumped around drowned out further words of apology. I was silently expressing my gratitude to the Source of All Supply, as I noted that the check was no doubt the largest he had ever seen, since it more than equaled his annual salary.

A few years earlier, his business firm had begun a subsidiary aspect of business which had never paid a bonus in any profits before, nor did it ever again. The check arrived in the "nick of time," since the bank hours permitted Saturday morning transactions. The flight tickets were scheduled for pick-up or cancellation the next day.

Karen's dad was witnessing their incredible jubilation as she realized that he needed an explanation. "Dad, I've got the passport and the reservations, and my bags are packed, ready to go with Emily Monday. Mom said if God intended to allow us to share the trip, we had to have faith as 'we dug the ditches.' So we prepared everything to be ready."

"But your mom didn't know that the check was going to be provided," he answered.

"Dad, that's what makes faith work, just trusting God to take care of filling the trenches that we dig. What better proof can there be than a gift from out of nowhere in our logical expectations?"

A Tour Review

When I first met Gladys Davis, we recognized each other from a number of past encounters. There was an immediate kinship since she, too, had clung to her old "trunks and passports" from past lives. Actually, a lot of the Cayce pioneer clan had brought in their memories as well, so our initial reunions were celebrations at the regrouping events.

Early in our friendship, Gladys and I exchanged stories of our family backgrounds, finding amusement in the parallels of country living. Since so many of our siblings, cousins, aunts, uncles and friends had the same names, we laughed about the name books our parents and grandparents must have exchanged. Similar social and church events were familiarly remembered, although about four hundred miles and a couple of decades separated our points of entry during this present era. Our relationship required no props or pretense. We were playmates, enjoying mutual interests and the fun of each other's re-encounters. Our families were mutually shared, especially when she took vacation time from work and spent it in our home, or I would visit "Glad Niche" to visit with her family.

Gladys and I were drawn together, not because of similarities of personalities, but in answer to a need that required diversification. The contrast was significant in our mutual need to serve. She supplied the cream. I churned it. Then, she gleaned the butter to spread on life's plain bread and we shared with everyone at the table. As teammates we enjoyed our games.

Like Diogenes, I had wandered around, looking for samples of untarnished adult purity for guides. Luckily, I found a few. Most of them were beyond my reach. Gladys recognized my struggle and stooped to help me rise. Her humility allowed no one to pass by her with needs unattended. Vigilance steered her mission to care for the lambs and lions and their survival in Peace with one another. Her Aquarian pitcher never ran dry of gentle-flowing kindness.

Through the years of visiting the old Hospital Building, the joy of observation from the vantage point of its hilltop premises renewed the mystique I had felt on my initial visit. As its residents magnetized friendships which spanned life memories for me, I found it necessary to make the rounds among them from the basement vault and therapy center to the sanctuary of Ruth Lenoir's "Upper Room." If I entered by climbing the dual front steps to the veranda that stretched around its main floor, my head bowed in salute toward the Library on the right, then flipped my view toward the "Information" window on my left, an official greeter framed behind a ledged shelf on the wall might be Mae Gimbert St. Clair or another familiar staffer.

Locating the whereabouts of people, places of interest, housing, food, therapy, study, or connecting with local members, they served us in the era that long preceded mobile phones and laptop computers. Looking back, I remember it as a period between candles, or kerosene lamps, and the LED lights that flash today's information portals on computers. It brings recall of the warm comfort of sharing live contact with touchable human beings.

I could barely exchange greetings before hearing the voice of Lydia J. Schraeder Gray booming from above, "I hear that Micki person. Tell her I'm waiting." That was my clue to get on upstairs, pronto. She must have monitored the parking lot below from her apartment window to see who was coming, or maybe she sensed the change in vibrations as different souls moved near her territory. Nothing could escape Lydia's perception, it seemed. Hers was a force with which to be reckoned, as Hugh Lynn and others were well aware. She had come from New Orleans to join the Cayce household, as a caretaker of Mrs. Cayce through the last months of her life, and, desiring to serve their legacy, remained to aid A.R.E. Her generosity and influence was immeasurable. Few people knew that her "Numerology Reading Contributions" were donated to the furnishings of the whole building and the beautification of the surrounding landscape.

Being upstairs meant that I paid my respects to Lydia, the official "House-Mother," giving her an update on my daughter's reason for not accompanying me and getting the latest news of "my Lorraine," as she always identified her niece, and her husband, Eric Jensen. After a gracious tea and cookie visit, I could continue my rounds with "Little Olive" Landers, a different power-house. Olive personified the expression, "Dynamite comes in small packages." Her editorials were pungent intellectual stimulants. She could digest a book of Auspinsky's writing, condense its essence to the perfume of a paragraph which even a classroom dunce could absorb with understanding. Now, that's potency!

Rising to the upper floor meant a wispy encounter with "The White Brotherhood," in the gentle presence of Ruth Lenoir, Prayer Secretary of the first Search for God study group, who chose the Affirmations and prayers to be printed as guidelines of monthly dedications. For years, her apartment served as a meeting place for the ongoing Number 1 Prayer Group, the "Glad Helpers." She entertained visitors from "flying saucers" to impromptu appearances of the Holy Mother. I know by experience that such visitations occurred even on the brightest days of summer, because I witnessed a few such events where she showed no sign of surprise.

After she had completed her book, *When the Last Trumpet Sounded,* I visited her. Having known her for years, I was touched by her look of utter depression and a frailty that I had never seen before. She welcomed me as warmly as ever, but began with her sad news as we sat on her sofa. "Hugh Lynn has told me that my book cannot be published after all. You know he has always said that if I could finish it, A.R.E. would print it. You and Harriet Williamson have helped me so much in getting it edited and inspired. So many have helped me, and now he says that it can't be done."

My Irish dander rose, "He can't do that, Ruth. He promised. He can't back out, now. Ruth, don't you worry any more. He's gotta fulfill his promise! Your book is going to be published!" I was really irked, but I wanted to reassure her as gently and firmly as possible. Then, suddenly an alcove of a dormer window blazed with a light so brilliantly white that I had to cover my eyes. Turning my head to look at Ruth, I saw her face glow as it mirrored the light. She was smiling, with a color in her cheeks, appearing as though the lines that had marked the passage of time across her face were erased by youthful energy. A transformation I could never have imagined was enveloping both of us. The presence was sensed as vibrational for me, but too bright for my visual discernment. I could not detect facial features, only form. Nor could I verify the amount of time that the apparition appeared. Ruth turned to me, still aglow, though the light had moved on. "Did you hear what the Holy Mother said?" I just waited. "She said, 'Micki speaks the truth, Ruth. Your book will be published soon.'"

I gave Ruth a farewell hug and made a beeline for Hugh Lynn's office. Passing by Noreen Leary, his faithful secretary, I entered his open door. He was pushing back from his desk to stand so I put my hand on his shoulder. "Stay put, Hugh Lynn, I just left Ruth. The Holy Mother visited us and said that you would be publishing her book as you had promised. If there is a problem with financing it, I am sure that there are many willing to help defray its expense."

Trying to describe his reaction after so many years have passed, I can only evaluate my delayed surprise that he made no effort to question the integrity of my announcement. He sort of shook his head with a resigned acceptance, "If the Holy Mother says it will be published, then, it will be published." Further discussion on the subject, I do not recall. I remember that within a short time, the book was autographed by Ruth and sent out to those who ordered copies. Recently I ran across a letter in my files from Phyllis Embleton (another super-lady-employee) apologizing that they had sent my copy before Ruth had a chance to sign it. If I would return it, she would replace it with a signed copy. For me, that was unnecessary. Sharing Ruth's visitation was an ample autograph for me. Sharing her joy of completion of an earthly project before joining the realm of angelic souls was great.

Gladys' cubby-hole office was in the basement, where the precious files were housed at that time. Because I would have planned ahead to share her lunch break, I would let her know that I was on the premises before visiting the therapists working on the "Foundation Floor" as I identified it. Since Edgar Cayce spent his earlier years giving physical Health Readings, emphasizing balance of physical, mental and spiritual nature, I felt that the root of the A.R.E. "tree of knowledge" was its physical therapy department. When some of its vital functions were closed after Gladys died, I was distressed that its roots were damaged.

Among the therapists in the basement of that white Temple on the hill, Avrum Levine labored with Dr. Reilly's therapeutic massage techniques. My years of his friendship renewed memories of our "Big Band" era of the 1940s and fifties, when he was a New York musician and I had a short stint there as a singer. Time out for me during a career in medicine, the show-biz world was an oasis of swaying palms and torsos, away from the bogs of tending physical pains.

Avrum's recall of Gladys during one of our last chats was labeling her as a "computerized memory of every Reading detail, as she tamed the atmospheric pressure of the building through her daily presence. By enticing smiles to appear on everyone's face in greeting her, all were prepared to face the world in the spirit of constructive service." I like his summary of her *persona*.

He shared a memory where one day Gladys had an auto accident on her way to work, so a police officer came to hear her version of its details. Acknowledging her fault in crossing traffic that she had failed to see coming was not easy for her to express. Temptation to cover her error was overwhelming, so that the gentleness of the policeman who sought her testimony relieved her emotional anxiety when he did not lead her off to jail in handcuffs. Avrum enjoyed the humility she exhibited in accepting the responsibility of an error in discernment, as a weakness of all earthlings, under a blanket of excuses. He saw her flustered, indicating that her feet touched the ground just like the rest of us earth beings, without the cushions of levitation which he assumed accounted for her extra height. Because she always made us feel taller, he had a new appreciation for her talent of seeing us eye-to-eye, as human as the rest of us on this plane.

Adoring her as a dear friend for many years as he did, I found his choice of this incident as a standout in appreciating that human bond of compassion.

Among many others trained by Dr. Harold Reilly are therapists of innate healing talents enhanced by his magic touch. Dr. Reilly was one of Edgar Cayce's most valuable assets as a friend whose generosity continued to bless the Work throughout his long life. Through the legacy of many trained students, his School of Massotherapy continues to enlist such specialists. When Bob Hope praised "The Life of Reilly" for his own longevity on Johnny Carson's show, I felt a special kinship with his appreciation of Dr. Reilly's help. His book on Drugless Therapy greatly benefits those who apply his advice. His special student, Sandra Duggan, through her colon care and therapy book, blesses many residents and visitors of Virginia Beach. Lorraine Lipani's healing hands were among the sessions I love to remember, and I am grateful for her contribution about Gladys, and Jeanie Dodd's, too. They were among Gladys' favorite caretakers.

*Dr. Genevieve Haller, a pioneer in the Work of Edgar Cayce
and the medical Readings, with Micki Kluge.*

Jeanie Dodd looked through her old journals to enhance her memories of sharing Gladys' presence as she massaged her regularly. A mutual friend had mentioned some events of Gladys as having forecast certain situations from her dream revelations. Among them was the name of Jeanie's future husband, so I asked if she recalled that. She did not, but she did say, "I went to see Gladys about my confusion on whether or not it is okay to pray for a relationship to work out. She said, "Yes," but to pray for the best to be brought to each of us. It is even okay to use his name with that stipulation that the best for each be done. She makes me feel so good. I love Gladys." This was written in her journal. Jeanie sent pictures of her wedding, which Gladys attended, and snapshots of her daughter.

A tribute to Gladys from Lorraine Lipani follows.

So many great women shaped the matrix of the Edgar Cayce Foundation. Most did not publish articles and books, and most did not have offices with their names on the doors. They rolled up their sleeves and did whatever had to be done to keep things running smoothly. They are the unsung heroes, loving and hard-working, that held the web together. Then there was Gladys—she was such a woman, as well as the keystone of the Foundation, and someone who trusted intuitively in the validity of the Readings.

When I moved to Virginia Beach in 1971, fresh out of college, there was not yet the new library and conference center, just the old Hospital Building and a lecture hall. The cozy library was on the first floor, just off the veranda. It was all rather homey, with a coffee machine in the bookshop, lots of folks reading or chatting about the Readings. Inevitably, the veranda was where the younger crowd would gather in the evenings—ostensibly to decipher some particularly cryptic Reading—but actually just to hang out with interesting friends.

Gladys would often stop and chat with us on her way out. She would readily offer a Reading by number that she thought would say something clarifying. She was easy around young people (though not always amused, like the time we told her one of us had discovered that, if you took enough Tonic 636, you could see yellow auras around everything).

Was Gladys psychic? It seemed to me that that generation who had actually been with Edgar was extremely cautious about displaying psychic ability themselves, or claiming such. They were more apt to simply zap the pants off you in a prayer group. Go figure.

I personally found Gladys deeply intuitive. As a young masseuse at the A.R.E. Therapy Department, I was delighted to find myself on the same floor as Gladys (that would be the ground floor of the old Hospital Building with plumbing pipes on the ceiling. As I say, the place was homey back then). Gladys came frequently for spa and massage treatments and would point me to certain Readings that I found invaluable in deepening my understanding of holistic health care. I will say that Gladys had a big hand in shaping my vision of the multidimensional human being. Thank you, Gladys!

The story I'd like to share is actually a very human one about Gladys. Sometime in the mid-1970s, before the new library building was built, Gladys ran off at lunchtime and married Les Wilmore. All the A.R.E. staff were abuzz with the news, and we waited on the veranda of the old hospital building for their return. We [later] showered them with (natural brown long grain) rice and teased Les about finally getting Gladys to marry him. How did he do it?

Gladys with Les Wilmore, 1979

We all knew Les had been trying to get his foot inside Gladys' house for years. He made himself handy at fixing things around the property. Gladys maintained her focus on the work of indexing the Readings for a soon to be computerized version. Actually before the CD-ROM, Gladys herself was the most accurate index of the Readings.

At any rate, Les had tired of waiting for Gladys to treat him as other than a volunteer handyman and went away for a few weeks. Gladys said something like, much to her surprise, she missed his being around all the time. Finally, she thought that it was worse to be without him than it was to put up with him. Les just stood there by her side, rocking on his heels. He wore his cowboy hat tilted a little and a big grin creased his face.

Les Wilmore, an Oklahoma transplant from Will Roger's territory with similar witty nature, had known Gladys for most of his years at Virginia Beach. He had endeared himself as a long-time friend and willing handyman for all of her widowed friends. He had been married, divorced and owned a few parcels of property in the area. Known as a fun character who brought an interesting philosophical twist to any serious question, he finally talked Gladys into renting him a

My daughter, Karen, with Ruth Burks

118

room of her home. Helping to keep the little cottage and lawn in good repair also added the social comfort of avoiding loneliness as the years wore on. That worked well for a little while.

When they decided to get married, though, everyone was surprised. She went to work that morning, all dressed up and, as she was leaving for lunch, she told her secretary, Gail Cayce, that she might not return that afternoon. They went to the Princess Anne County Court House on February 10, 1976, where they had arranged with a Justice of the Peace to have a short ceremony, his wife acting as a witness signing the legal documents. Virginia Beach had not yet been merged with the County and the Court House area had not been adorned with all the surrounding facilities that are now part of its complex.

After exchanging vows, they made a phone call to Hugh Lynn to announce their news. "He was flabbergasted," Gladys told me later, "but asked to speak with Les." Hugh Lynn congratulated Les as having won the hand of the Queen of Virginia Beach, and being his "adopted sister," he probably offered some brotherly advice as well. Since there were no restaurants nearby, Les asked his new bride where they should go. She suggested that they visit Karen, my daughter, who was renting a house-trailer on his farm nearby.

A few minutes later, they knocked on Karen's door. She had just made a pot of tea and placed her uncut cheesecake on her table, so she welcomed them to share refreshments as they beamed their news which Gladys wished her to call and let me know about. She also called Gail to announce that, having just married Les, she planned to take the rest of the day off. Their surprise was no longer a secret from their world of friends, as the A.R.E. staff members responded with enthusiasm to celebrate their union. A reception party was soon celebrated in their honor at Headquarters by their friends.

Gladys had intended to avoid any fanfare, and official changes in adding "Wilmore" to the printing expenses of the organization's literature. As Guardian of the Cayce legend, Archivist, Historian, and Corporate Secretary of the combined facilities of the Edgar Cayce Foundation, Atlantic University, A.R.E.'s Board of Directors, she felt "Gladys Davis Turner" was sufficient identification to her role in the Work. Les Wilmore was elated and content to share her life as a partner in their home with "free rent" and bliss. Now that is practicality enough for him.

When little Michael learned of their marriage, he asked her if Les would continue to pay his rent money since he would still be living there. She told him that as her husband, paying rent would no longer be necessary. She thoroughly enjoyed sharing Michael's response, "Granny, I thought you were smarter than to make a deal like that."

Less One Rooster

When I think back during those years that Gladys shared with Les, Karen lived in his house trailer off Sandbridge Road on his farm. It was located in a field, seemingly miles from nowhere, which suited her purpose at the time. As a freelance artist, painter and illustrator, she enjoyed the frugality of its less costly rent and food. Raising her own vegetables and chickens meant fresh eggs daily, outdoor exercise, less grocery shopping time and more privacy to concentrate on the use of her talents without having to rent a studio.

When she decided to take a summer semester course of sculpting in New York, she arranged to have a neighbor take care of her pets and property. I would be there during Pat's vacation week. Thirty years away from farm life as I had known growing up was challenging to reorient to chores that were never among my favorite occupations. I could appreciate privacy as one who grew up in an overpopulated house, but chose city dwelling since leaving home for college as a teenager. Isolated living quarters seemed an exorbitant price for a practical diet or to be left alone.

The garden area was fenced in to protect it and the chickens from wild varmints. A shelter containing poles for roosting at night and a row of straw-filled nests to invite the eggs for gathering daily. Water troughs and feeders that needed refills weekly, at least, were placed inside and around the coop. When I had difficulty locating the pump switch, I called Les for directions and as a notice of my arrival. He graciously extended a welcome to call him for any help that I might require, waiting online to be sure that I got the water running through the garden hose. In assuring him that the pump was on and operational, I reminded him that Gladys and I expected him to go out to dinner with us the next evening.

I dragged the hose through the garden gate and closed it behind me as the lone rooster stood nearby, peering intently. He strutted toward me with

a belligerent air of defiance. I greeted him as "Roscoe," since Karen had a knack for naming all of her pets. For example, a German Shepherd derivative she once had was named "Argus," in honoring the giant with a hundred eyes whom Hermes had killed and then placed the eyes on the feathers of a peacock's tail. He was her devoted friend and watchdog. Since she consistently utilized Greek mythological characters, I realized that I should have checked on this one, as this cocky little rooster did not respond warmly to my alias for him. "Roscoe" bristled with his sense of authority as I entered the henhouse with the hose in hand. As I focused on the trough being filled, he attacked me from the rear, slashing my slacks with his extended spurs. Feeling the sharp pain as blood soaked my ripped pants, I whirled to shoot him with a full blast of water. He would barely retreat before sailing back toward me. I chased him around the coop a few times, screaming a rare collection of other aliases that accompanied my emotions, until I spotted a sapling pole by the fence gate. Reaching to grasp a tool with which I could slaughter the evil little monster, my feet skidded on the flood-soaked path, rocketing my body toward a slamming thud in a pool of the organic mud that fertilized her generous garden. The earth quaked and he skittered out of sight behind the henhouse. I could have sworn I heard him laughing as I moaned with agony.

Gradually, I picked myself up and hobbled out the gate, dragging the spewing hose to the faucet to close the valve. Fury overwhelmed my pain as I shelled out of the muddy clothes and cleaned my spur-slashed thighs and bruised torso. The rage lingered as I dialed Les' number and shared a replay of the battle. "Could you help me catch that demonic rooster? I've got to kill him, if I'm going to tend Karen's garden and hens!"

Les managed to be solemn as he asked if I had broken any bones or needed any medical attention. When I assured him that I was physically intact, he could hold back no longer. He had to laugh, and I found myself laughing with him, but I knew that one of us had to go. "You know that Karen loves that rooster, and he's probably tired of waiting for her to get back home. I'll catch him for you, but I don't want her mad at me."

I promised to take full responsibility, so he promptly came and, without assistance, caught that feathered monster and roped his feet together. He checked again to be sure that I didn't want him. "Okay then, I'll see if Miss Gladys will cook us some chicken and dumplin' stew."

"Mean as he is, Les, that'll be the toughest bird she ever cooked," I said.

"She will know how to do it. Having put up with me, she can easily tenderize any bird." With a smile of sheer pride, he drove away with the little red rooster in his truck with my indebted gratitude following.

When Gladys later described Les' appreciation of her culinary masterpiece, she said that she did not know which he enjoyed the most, the stew or the story I had added to his repertoire of nature's elements. As he reiterated it, he called it his latest "cocktale." We laughed and laughed.

Les adored the ground Gladys walked on and kept her entertained. When he died August 6, 1982, his memorial service was attended by many of their long-time friends. I have never heard more laughter during such an event, as Gladys allowed his letters to her be read by a friend, and so many impromptu speakers shared their memories of his escapades. His humor often triggered some depths of concerns worth pondering that touch hearts and minds in ways which leave lasting impressions for consideration. Edgar Cayce often counseled that hearty laughter was a healing force. Les Wilmore had spread the opportunity to indulge humor through some creative angles of viewing life through his lens of individuality.

Even on his final trip to the hospital, he kept his sense of humor as sharp as ever. When his physician expressed serious concerns over the grave diagnoses of numerous organs, Les looked toward Gladys. Her concern for him was lining her solemn countenance. Les turned toward the respected doctor, "Thank you for all of your conscientious care, Sir, but I refuse to die of fright." For those friends who had understood his brand of levity, we shared Gladys' hearty appreciation of it and her understanding tolerance for his tendency to fall off the wagon occasionally.

PART FOUR

Another Glance in the Rear View Mirror

Back when Gladys was adjusting after her move with the Cayce family to Dayton, Ohio, the shifts in lifestyle were as drastic for her as the seismic movements of the Earth's crust. The world of mental ideas and physical travel opened through contact with their new clientele. Her introduction to the sophistication of New York's cosmopolitan ambience came through her first encounter with Morton Blumenthal's mother, who lovingly advised Gladys to take life less seriously as a counterbalance to her committed service to the Work. Mrs. Blumenthal saw the dignity of her dedication to Edgar Cayce's focus on the application of spiritual laws as a worthy cause. She said that Gladys should also lighten her outlook on the foibles of human nature, allowing herself the luxury of amusement, else her anxiety for the welfare of others might become too heavy for her gentle soul. Spotlighting Mr. Cayce's ability to enjoy the humor of comedic routines as a balancing agent, she encouraged both Gladys and Gertrude to relax and pamper themselves more. Mrs. Blumenthal was a wise woman, further evidenced by the success of her exceptionally brilliant sons who helped establish Edgar Cayce in Virginia Beach.

As a highly-regarded mentor, Gladys adopted Mrs. Blumenthal's sage advice through a more relaxed approach to her duties, allowing herself to respond with her own genuine sense of amusement. So, as Gladys matured in her nurturing duties of family and career, she managed to incorporate laughter in abundance, while never compromising her level of service. Computerizing the Readings, while indulging us clowns, rejuvenated her fountain of youth.

William Hall shared this memory of an impromptu encounter with her:

> Back in 1981, walking up the spiral staircase within the A.R.E. Visitor Center, I spied Gladys at the top. She waited until we were at the highest tread, her eyes intent upon the winter-swaddled infant. She lit up with even more than with her usual effervescent demeanor, exclaiming in her sweet Alabama voice, "Just look, another Edgar Cayce Baby!"

The stern earthiness in response using my overly protective paternal voice was, "Now, Ms. Gladys, don't start those rumors. You certainly know the kind of people we attract here. This happens to be a William Charles Hall baby."

Pulling her leg that day is one of the fondest memories I have of her, as she backed up, stuttering, "I mean… I mean…"

"Of course, I am pulling your leg, Ms. Gladys. I know that you were referring to my earnestness in following the Readings, as I had prayed for the highest soul I was worthy of helping into this world, as I delivered this first son at the National Congressional Cemetery Gatehouse, of all places." Gladys must have loved babies, 'cause she wanted more out of us. I asked her to place her hand on the baby's fontanel, telling her of our Cherokee belief that wisdom would be transferred to Raphael Alexander Hall, and she would receive a few more days. She enjoyed hearing this, and said, "What a special baby." We both laughed easily. People should know this about her, her warmth and her sense of humor, even if the brunt of the joke was on her.

Allen Van Lehn of Livermore, California, wrote about a memory from the 1970s when he had attended a conference at Virginia Beach, VA. As most participants were likely to do, he stayed at the Marshall's Hotel on the oceanfront off Atlantic Avenue, which was owned and operated by A.R.E. members. Meals and Meditation were among the magnets that drew many fellow members into discussions that launched extended friendships back into relationships that bridged past, present and future concerns. His association with Hugh Lynn Cayce, Herb and Meredith Puryear, Everett Irion, Shirley Winston, Bob and Anne Clapp and other staffers was a bonus treat of that era. Allen commented:

> One day, I was walking up the driveway toward the back of the Hospital Building when I was joined by Gladys. Even though she was about twice my age, she nearly outpaced me. She was very friendly, introducing herself and then asking me my name and where I was from. After asking what brought me to Headquarters, how I was introduced to the A.R.E., she asked me what it was about the Cayce material that most attracted me. I answered without hesitation, the great wealth

of religious information. I have a great affinity for the information and people around the time of Jesus. She seemed quite pleased with my answer and surprised me with what I consider one of the highest highlights of my life: a kiss on my right cheek! Oh, I eventually washed that cheek, but the memory has never faded and never been washed away.

Toni Romano, among our treasured leaders in Outreach Services, sent this comment by Kenneth Klein:

> One time, when I was at the A.R.E. in Virginia Beach over thirty years ago, I got the idea that Readings given by Edgar Cayce on the day that I was born might have special significance for me. When I came upon Gladys in the old Headquarters Building, I asked her if it would be possible to locate the Readings given on 10/15/37. She simply went upstairs and came back down in a few minutes with a notebook, telling me Readings #1458-1 and #1459-1 were given on that date. I then needed to go over to the library and copy the two Readings from the appropriate binders on the shelf. They were a Life Reading and a Physical Reading for two different individuals. Nowadays, such a search can be done by a computer, but Gladys' notebooks were just as efficient.

Typical of her organized efficiency, this note records a facet of her organizational expertise and file retrieval ability. Retaining the shorthand pads and her diary notes of the years as Edgar's chief scribe, had made it possible to retrieve the exact words as originally transcribed when the files would otherwise have been lost, as the rats had chewed and defiled the pages of the broken cabinet when it was discarded on the woodpile after Mr. Cayce's funeral. As an archivist, the devoted attention to details of her expertise was unsurpassed. Otherwise, their parallel mission may have ended as in eras of history when destroyed by succeeding rulers of those ancient cultures or some kind of Theodora-clone eraser. Even an avid "Translator" desiring to "modernize the scripts" of Cayce's "archaic concepts and language" to fit a crude version of undisciplined lingo, or code of loose ethics, could undo the value of her work. Though we have the technological capacity to conserve records of our modern events and concepts, future calamities and perceptual alterations could obliterate the traces she preserved for us. The Akashic Records remain indestructible, though inaccessible by most ordinary souls.

Among the staff that served A.R.E. so well in sharing their dedication to the preservation of Edgar Cayce's Readings for posterity were other very efficient souls, magnetized by their kinship of spiritual nature and talents. As co-workers during Gladys' tenure, their appreciation for her was rewarded in having close proximity through their years of service. Paying tribute to her by sharing memories for this book, I am blessed by the special friendships they represent as mutual bonds of our association.

Gladys at A.R.E. Headquarters with the archives of the Edgar Cayce Readings.
Photo courtesy of the Edgar Cayce Foundation.

In answering my call for medallions of memory out of the years of knowing Gladys and working on the premises of A.R.E., Alma L. Crovatt chose to recount these two vignettes:

> *Event 1:* In 1972 I was asked to be a volunteer and work in the Braille Library. Many today do not know that the A.R.E. had a small library with free loan books and tapes for use by the visually impaired. There were several certified Braille writers and many qualified readers, all producing the Edgar Cayce material in a form the blind could use for healing and enlightenment. It was during this period that I first met Gladys. She often told us the work for the blind was "wonderful." On my birthday each year afterward, she would send a card of appreciation for our work for the blind. Gladys said she thought that many visually handicapped people could receive hope and help by hearing what Cayce had written for others. Her spirit of wanting to help people, no matter what their problems, would always touch my heart when I was in her presence.
>
> *Event 2:* There was a Work Readings group meeting before work once a week and since Gladys led the group, I wanted to be part of it. It was wonderful to hear of her many experiences with "Mister Cayce" and a blessing to have with us the secretary who took the notes and knew exactly what the past activities were pertaining to the Work Readings. I can still see that cute smile on her face and hear the little laughs she gave after sharing something she mis-said or did. Her presence in the group impressed on me that Love was a big part of Edgar Cayce's gift to the world, and our Gladys was the designated soul to demonstrate how to give it to others. She did this beautifully and I will always remember her and smile.

Alma was also "cut from the same bolt of cloth," using my mother's term again. I was saddened to see her retire, but it is great that she is applying her time to art, creating tiles, and enjoying family.

When I think of all the members who joined the staff in services provided to share the Work around the world as interest mounted, many individuals, such as Judith, stand out as experts. In the Glad Helpers tradition, she was a bridge of support when Nell Clairmonte took over the Search for God group work when Elsie Secrist joined her husband Bill as world-traveling A.R.E. representatives. She formed a program, "Over the Wall," sharing books and workers with prisons across the country to help inmates study, pray and meditate which is still a vibrant aid to many.

This is the contribution to our reflections of Gladys by Judith Stevens, A.R.E.'s *poet laureate* of the Search for God Groups:

Ode To The Quiet One

A grown woman when I met her,
Whose laugh was as irrepressible as that of a young girl,
Gladys Davis Turner was always turning heads
With her towering, yet unassuming presence
    and the kindest blue eyes in the world
    that seemed to bid, "Welcome."
The Quiet One.
An unostentatious woman who picked up litter
    in the A.R.E. parking lot when it was yet unpaved,
    someone who taped her weekly study group
    discipline on the outside of her serviceable
    black purse and carried with her everywhere
    the current Glad Helpers' prayer list.
A woman who had a kind of radar
    that detected someone else's pain at fifty paces
    and was ready to meet it with love—
An ageless, timeless woman who was drawn to children
    and young people
    who picked up countless hitchhikers
    that she sweetly brought to our Monday night
    group meeting for a gentle rehabilitation.
The Quiet One.
All those years of protecting the Readings,
Protecting Mr. and Mrs. Cayce,

Putting her own life on "hold" to be available
   whenever they needed
   (though she would be the first to tell you that
   her life became the Cayce family and the Readings
   and that she was carried along on the current of the
   times, discovered her life's work and never
   looked back).
Postponing marriage, realizing she could not
   "serve two masters"
Foregoing children, caring for her brother's child and so
   many others
Childless, she was mother and grandmother to
   all she met, for love flows effortlessly to love.
The Quiet One.
Jotting notes in the margins of her *Search for God* book,
Ever the student, always seeking to correct, improve,
   learn, grow,
Making the Work ever more available to those who sought it
Measuring up to her Master's standard of perfection—
Gladys: The Quiet One.

Personalities that revved up the vibrations of the local headquarters were known as "live wires." Their voltage sparked an increase in keeping the place an attractive magnet for visitors from across the country to attend lectures and events of social and intellectual stimulation. Absorbing the ambience of mood and friendly environs was a soul-restorative process that inspired the desire of belonging which bonded our hearts and emotional ties to the family, or tribal, kinship. We carried the essence of its effect back home to share with others, infusing their desire to seek personal experiences that would match our benefits. As the membership grew, representatives from headquarters were invited to the hinterlands to touch those who could not travel to headquarters. So the organization expanded through those years.

Dancing with the "*joie de vie*" contagious to all who touched her native spirit, is one such special representative of that era. Now in her nineties, still full of vigor and joy is this contributor to our "string of pearls" collection of treasured memories. Geraldine (known as Jerry by most of us) McDowell shares this delightful note:

> When I came to work at A.R.E. I worked in the old building on the hill. I worked with Gladys in the Library Workroom in the basement where the therapy department is now. I was working at the Navy Base at night and at A.R.E. days. One day I was so sleepy, I fell asleep at the typewriter. They told me to go lie down on the old green couch in the hall, the same couch Edgar Cayce lay to do his Readings.
>
> When I woke up Mr. Cayce was standing beside me smiling down at me. He raised his hand putting his finger on my nose, I smiled up at him and he disappeared. I was so excited I rushed in the room and told Gladys, "I just saw Mr. Cayce in the hall."
>
> Gladys said, "I see him all the time. Did he say anything?"
>
> I said, "No, he just put his finger on my nose."
>
> Gladys said, "Jerry, he's picked you out and you'll never be able to leave."
>
> As soon as I could, I quit my job at the Base and worked in the Library. I was happy to find out that Gladys was like me and could see ghosts, too.

When Gladys started dating Les Wilmore, he would come and hang around and keep us laughing, he was so funny. He called Gladys his "sweet petunia" and he was crazy about her. Gladys said "Jerry, I guess I'll have to marry him, people are starting to talk." He left us laughing all the time.

We all loved to have Gladys tell about what a time they (the Cayces) had in making ends meet and how she and Gertrude worried and Edgar would just laugh and they always made it. When they would try to talk to him about it, he would just go fishing or out in the garden.

They always had company and people coming in and out. The bills kept coming in faster than the money and they got a letter saying if the electric bill wasn't paid that day, it would be turned off. Gertrude and Gladys told Edgar and he said "Don't worry, I'm going fishing."

When the mailman came they got a check for the exact amount of the bill, Gladys ran down to the office barefoot and in her apron and paid the bill.

When the new building was being built, we all had fun running up and down in the sand and watching it come together. When it was done I was standing with Hugh Lynn and Gladys out in front admiring it and Gladys said "I never thought I'd live to see it happen. All those years of struggling really paid off."

Friends & More Friends

Social events that kept Gladys sparkling were weddings, for many of which she served as a special Matron of Honor or Bridesmaid. Welcoming babies to our world was another joy she shared in blessing. No one I ever knew enjoyed dancing more than she did. Special events like the dance nights during Congress Week each summer helped to balance her intense focus on organizing the mountains of archival collections of Cayce's periphery. Maybe because her youth was so ingrained with too little play time, the highlights of her father's glow when he gathered his brood to attend the "hoedowns" where he fiddled and sang as everyone hugged and danced revived her spirits. Her old fashioned concept of requiring a partner to attend a dance meant that she was reluctant to appear without one, so my job was to push. "I will pick you up at seven" (or whatever appropriate time). She knew that I would be alone, and did not want me to miss the event; thus, duty prevailed.

That's where friends like Vic Reiffer, Ken Ackley and many others shined their brightest in allowing her to fully enjoy the social events that came so rarely in her busy schedule. Vic, especially, touched her heart through the last decade of her life. He showered her with greeting cards that kept her humor intact, bringing healthy laughter that she could share with all who trespassed the Edgar Cayce Foundation Department, since they were displayed as her decor specialty. Having a taste of Vic's generous spirit available had an impact that bonded her natural capacity to appreciate all phases of the Work, from the preposterous to the sublime. Among those dearest to her, Vic remains one of my favorites, and I feel particularly grateful that his friendship has continued to boost my morale through the ensuing years, underscored by the accompanying love of his wonderful partner, Celeste.

In one of the Readings, Cayce encouraged everyone to enjoy laughter as healing; a good joke, or even a raunchy one, was recommended. From the instigator of all the laughs Vic provided for Gladys is his sincerely expressed memoir note copied here in behalf of all who know her role as "the Angel Gladness." That includes Irene Harrison (#1158 formerly Ruth, sister of Jesus) who often used that title for her when we discussed many references about her.

Vic Reiffer's comment for sharing our memories:

> In 1979 I was selected from the Philadelphia council to represent them at the 1979 congress. It was my first time at A.R.E.
>
> There were sharing groups set up. I saw in another group an older woman and asked, "Who is that lady?" They told me, "That's Gladys Davis."
>
> I excused myself and walked over to the other group and asked if I could join them and was accepted. This group was right under the window of the control room.
>
> I couldn't believe that I was actually seeing and talking to the woman that knew Edgar Cayce and wrote down the Readings. I had met Hugh Lynn the year before at a seminar

in Pennsylvania and was thrilled. But I was enthralled with Gladys. I was so impressed with this famous woman being so gentle and kind. She seemed to have no ego; she treated everyone as special, including me.

Later that week I was elected Congress Chairman for 1980.

When I got home I was exited about having the honor of being the 1980 Congress chairman, but I was overwhelmed by the fact that I actually met Gladys Davis. I wanted to show how much I appreciated meeting her, so I sent her a "mushy" thank you card. I normally don't send these type of cards but I wanted her to know how much I thought of her.

Shortly after I got a nice letter from her. I was reading many Cayce books and remembered that we are all the same soul age just different bodies in time. So the next time I went to the store I saw some funny cards and started to send them to her, always respectful but still a little ornery. Every time I would go in a store I would find funny cards and send them. This went on for months.

As Congress Chairman, I had no idea how to run a Congress and just followed my heart, trying to do my best. There were some ideas I wanted to try.

Before I went to Congress I did not know there was one. There was no general knowledge unless you were in the "old timer" set.

So I wanted to start a Congress update article in the A.R.E. news that went to all members. I believed that ANY A.R.E. member that pays a membership fee should be entitled to come and participate in their Congress.

Mark Thurston was the liaison between Congress and staff. I believe it was about November of 1979 when I decided to go to A.R.E. to talk to Mark Thurston about the $1,500 per year budget and my ideas.

When I got there I wanted to say "Hi" to Gladys and Jeannette Thomas. When I walked in the foundation door I was surprised. All along me top of the filing cabinets were the cards I had been sending. There were easily sixty cards. Gladys said she loved them and others on staff would stop in to see them when she got them. I continued to send them for years after. I guess I've sent over 300 cards.

Jeannette said that Gladys would ask her almost every day if she got any cards from Vic.

We became friends. I never went to her house. I wanted to visit her, but I felt she needed a home without people. All day long people were always trying to see her and she wouldn't turn them away.

1985 had been a rough year with bills, my car had a 120,000 miles on it and stress at work. I was worn out. I felt that I wasn't doing what I should be doing with the Cayce material, I was involved locally but I felt I should be doing more, like traveling, but had no money to do it. I was meditating and asked God to let me do the Cayce Work and travel, and if he made it possible, I would give out Cayce books wherever I went (planting seeds).

The next night I was driving home from a Cayce meeting and thinking to myself, I can have the house paid off in about eight years, a small voice in my head said "Why?" I couldn't come up with a good reason.

The mortgage interest rates were coming down. I told my wife what happened. She always liked to travel but was concerned. I said I'll apply to my credit union and if I can't get the money it means we shouldn't go. I applied. A few nights later I had a dream. In the dream I had money, I bought a minivan and traveled to Europe.

I woke up my wife and told her that we got approved . When she asked how I knew, I told her about the dream. I called the credit union and found that I had been approved. I took out $30,000 equity and re-mortgaged to a lower rate. It was just before the 1985 June Congress. My wife and I decided to go to Europe from Sept to Oct 17th, planned to buy a new minivan and take 4 weeks off from work.

I bought Cayce books and back-packed them to Europe, to do our part of my promise to God. At Congress I told CT (Dr. Charles Thomas Cayce, A.R.E.'s President, grandson of Gertrude and Edgar) what I planned on doing. He thought it was a good idea.

Bill Secrist heard about it and called me. I was in visiting Gladys. I answered the phone in the outer office and it was Bill. He was really upset and yelled, "Who gave you permission to do my job? I'm the International Rep." I was shocked and dumbfounded. I told him I'm not doing HIS job and acknowledged that he IS the International Representative, then told him goodbye politely. I was so shaken that Gladys asked me what happened. I told her that I don't even let my own father talk to me like that. And that I was going to write Bill a letter. She said "Darling, don't let it bother you. Bill has been like that for years. You know what to do. You just keep on keeping on."

1985 Congress. At the skit night, our son, Joshua sang to Gladys the old song "I'll Be Seeing You" and gave her a flower. He was only 4-1/2 but memorized that song on our six hour car trip to Congress. He thought Gladys was nice.

When I got home from that Congress, Gladys called to see if I was ok! Then she sent me a card reminding me with a Cayce quote about "keep on keeping on."

In September Les and I went to Europe and gave all the books away to libraries, groups and individuals. We even gave one to the Vatican and one to Prince Charles and got thank you letters from their representatives.

Throughout the years I have always used what she said in future things I did. If I felt it was the right thing to do I "kept on keeping on," no matter who disagreed with me, as long as it was not for my ego. Some things did not meet with approval from the A.R.E. crowd and I was rejected by a lot of the people whom I thought were my good A.R.E. friends. (Remember C.A.R.E.M. in 1987?) It hurt to think that my friends rejected me but I remembered that Gladys did all the work for years and was never realty appreciated. I was in good company.

1986. When Les and I heard Gladys was ill and was in the hospital we decided to drive down. Les couldn't leave for a week, Jeanette called me and said that Gladys was in a coma and the doctors didn't think she would last long, and if I wanted to see her that I better come soon. Les told me to fly down by myself. I left the next morning. Before I left I Xeroxed Josh's hand.

I walked into the hospital room and Gladys was awake and seemed really glad to see me. She had just come out of her coma-like state about an hour before. I gave her a kiss and hug from me, Les and Josh. Then gave her the Xerox of Josh's hand. I had bought a flower and put it in the Xerox so it looked like Josh had it in his hand. I told her Josh said, "Tell Gladys, 'I'll be seeing you.'"

We talked some and I started to tear up. Gladys was looking for something in her bed, and I asked her if I could help. She found what she was looking for, a tissue for me to wipe my eyes. I told her "Gladys, as sick as you are you still are helping others!" We talked a little more, then I told her, "I better let you get some rest." I kissed her and, as I was leaving, she said, "Tell Josh, 'I'll be seeing you.'" I blew a kiss to her and walked out into the hall with tears in my eyes. That was the last time I saw her.

She was a special soul I tell people that to me, Gladys was the embodiment of the Christ Spirit.

In 1997 I was in the hospital to take out a broken pacemaker lead that was causing me to cough blood. I was rushed to the hospital to have open heart surgery to cut my heart open to remove this wire from my heart and pulmonary artery. There was a good chance that I wouldn't survive. As I was being prepped for surgery, I knew there was a good chance I wouldn't make it. I did not pray to God or Jesus or ask for my dead grandparents for help. I said quietly "Gladys if it's my time, I hope you will be there to help me over!" This is how much I thought of this special soul.

Gladys with wings.
Photo courtesy of the
Edgar Cayce Foundation.

Vic has lots of company in counting on her expertise in levitating her adoring followers through "God's other door" since she lifted our spirits so often while in physical touch.

My granddaughter, Alexis, summarized this recorded response to our inquiry with these memories of Gladys during a memorable visit with the last survivor of the original Edgar Cayce Foundation members. We treasure his long friendship as a link to the man we cherish as Teacher of Truth. Born in February of 1919, Edgar Evans Cayce, youngest son of Gertrude and Edgar Cayce, was almost five years old when Gladys joined their family in moving from Selma, Alabama, to Dayton, Ohio. Growing up with her as "an elder sister" meant that his closeness to her was conditioned by the comfort of her presence as normally subjective, rather than having the objective of outsiders looking in. In his nineties, he epitomizes the genteel man as a product of ideal parental infusion of their loving expertise from every angle. He symbolizes the results of an ideal home atmosphere. He and his beautiful wife, Katherine, occupying the house they built as their first home, are icons of harmony and stability in this turbulent world of the fledgling twenty-first century. Reflecting the values his parents promoted, he stands as a beacon among us as an honorable soul.

Alexis remarked, "My grandmother and I met Edgar Evans Cayce in Virginia Beach at the house where he and his wife Katherine have lived since 1947. The great old pine trees in the front yard stand as a testament to the Cayces' long residence there."

Edgar Evans began telling us about his father and his relationship with the Readings:

> "He [Edgar Cayce] was giving Readings in Kentucky, before I was born, and people started asking him questions in the Readings about who was going to win the ball game, or the horse race, or what'll happen in the stock market. He would answer them, but when he woke up, he just didn't feel right. He'd have headaches or feel sick in the stomach. He knew something was wrong and when he realized what it was, that they were making money on the suggestions. He thought that he was supposed to help people, but he wasn't supposed to do that kind of stuff. So he said, "I'm through with all this, I'm leaving!" and he moved his family to Selma, Alabama, and opened a photographic studio. He gave up

giving Readings, and he didn't start again until Hugh Lynn [lost his eyesight in a small explosion in the studio]. The doctors wanted to take out one eye and said he'd probably never see again, so he asked Dad for a Reading. Dad gave him a Reading, and it told what do to save the eye. After a couple of weeks, a big scab came off and Hugh Lynn could see. So that got Dad back into the idea that maybe he ought to do Readings so he could help people."

"Of course it made headlines in the paper," said Edgar Evans laughing, "'Psychic Cures Son' and all that."

"He made a rule, though, that Mother [Gertrude] would be the one that would give him the suggestions in the Reading, ask the questions, so there wouldn't be anyone asking other questions. So that's the way it happened, and that's when Gladys joined the family. He needed someone to take it down in shorthand. They didn't have, you know, microphones and stuff like that then," he said smiling towards my mini digital recorder on the kitchen table. "He tried two or three people and Gladys was the best one at being able to take shorthand, and she fitted in real well. She became just like one of the family. She was almost like a sister, and she moved with us when we went to Dayton... That's when Dad got involved with the Blumenthals, and they supported building the hospital in Virginia Beach."

"I've known Gladys so long that I wouldn't know where to start telling you what I remember about her. She was a vital part of our lives. Gladys came in to do stenographic work; she was a real good stenographer. But it turned out that she had a memory like a computer. She could remember peoples' Readings from months back and years back, what the Reading was about, and what was suggested for it. She really fit in with the family because she got along with everyone really well. I mean she was an easy person to get along with. You know, she was interested in the Work, in the Readings, so she tried to transcribe them accurately, and you know I think she did a good job of it."

Edgar Evans Cayce identified Gladys as part of his closely knit family, and marvelled at her "computerized memory of all the details of each Reading," as we all do. He expressed his appreciation as if she were his own wise sister.

Generosity being a genetic trait of the whole Cayce clan, Alexis and I left with a stock of mementos, books and enhanced auras from their warm stimulation. Having known both Hugh Lynn and Edgar Evans through the years, I appreciated the praise for Gladys from her "adopted brothers" even more.

Recognition Recycled

When I first became involved with A.R.E., my psychic memory alerts returned with a vengeance as I met the "pioneers" who had been drawn back into the mission work of Edgar Cayce and Gladys Davis. Recognition was so prevalent among us. Because our association was so cooperative, I felt that I was back home with our beloved family of heavenly friends.

Decades later, although its members have moved in and out of the premises, the sense of family remains. Granted, the degrees of camaraderie vary in generational shifts, similar to the movement of tribes or caravans passing through the City of the Hills and Plains of Persia, on the streets of Rome, Jerusalem, Paris, or even groups of earlier pioneers and founders of America. Perhaps even without conscious individual recognition from former relationships, bonds of spiritual kinship are strongly sensed. Committed to the purpose of attuning ourselves and awakening others to express the joy of Belonging Together as one human race, we rejoice as we apply this opportunity in soul development.

Exemplifying selfless devotion in promoting Edgar Cayce's role of projecting God's messages as he received them, Gladys Davis recorded, transcribed and preserved *verbatim et literatim*, every jot and tittle. Totally lacking the intellectual arrogance or the egotistical insolence to alter the vocabulary of the message as Edgar Cayce delivered it, she guarded the language used.

Others pleaded that it was so archaic as to confuse later generations or "speed-readers" who had failed to study the King James version of Biblical Scriptures, which Cayce quoted most often. Gladys felt duty-bound to keeping the messages true to the source of Cayce's interpretation.

Commentaries were encouraged, allowing future generations leeway for analysis and expansion. Volumes in literary details are spawned in the tributaries, from *"There Is A River"* to the oceans of intellectual and spiritual response. Leaving the search for individual nuances of interpretation or understanding to each recipient, or group, the pioneers of this organization applied and analyzed the variety of material given. From synthesizing categories of information, they shared advice for healthy improvements of heart, mind and soul. Thus, like the ancient scrolls of the Torah, debate, research, discussion, meditation, insight, guidance and choice would be acquired according to the seeker's value system. Interpretations abound in diverse commentaries, but the initial record should be unabridged! As Pontius Pilate retaliated when asked to change the label he had given to attach to Jesus' cross "King of the Jews," "What I have written, I have written," or, "That's exactly what I meant to have said!" Each Reading was the truth as Cayce was able to convey of what God intended to be shared. His record speaks for itself. When you want a different version, set aside your own will and listen for it. Go Direct.

Gladys' palm.

144

Psychics come and psychics go, but Gladys knew the Source of Cayce's authority. She shared it and witnessed its proof throughout the 62-1/2 years of involvement with his Readings. Twenty-two years as his secretary and confidante was followed by over forty in establishing the Edgar Cayce Foundation and coordinating ways of using the material that she has preserved in the archives of A.R.E. During her latter years she promoted the launch of a twentieth century's technological triumph by overseeing that unadulterated copies of original messages would be transferred to CD-ROM for unlimited study of those accessing her records. Integrity was her ideal.

Her knowledge of each word that Cayce uttered was heard, understood, hand-written in shorthand, transcribed to the typewritten page, then reread for accuracy before sharing the copy with the patient, physician or client. Filing, re-copying, or sharing the content with Mr. Cayce, since he had no conscious awareness of it, she, more than anyone else in the chain of listeners, literally memorized each message. Inspired by them, though intended for others' use, she pondered their value in her own heart, mind and applicable usage as direct advice from God. "Waste not, want not," being a theory that permeated every aspect of her young life, she incorporated the admonitions to apply in shaping her wholeness. "Sunshine" magnified through Gladness penetrated her relationships as a natural result in fulfilling her soul's potential.

Reflection of her sunny disposition, imbued with total trust in God's Providence, the aura of the Eternal Christos, encased every aspect of her dedication to the legacy of their joint mission. Living each stage of develop-ment, as she believed worthy of God's Patience with all souls, she nurtured the benefits as she mastered the Work. Her challenges were not simply ease of accepting the platitudes of conventional hearsay, but confronting doubts and genuine fears of survival, criticisms of family and friends. The diseases, anxieties of grief, and war, poverty and gender power struggles quilted her years, just as others contend and overcome, using Grace and Mercy.

Humble through her gratitude for benevolent compassion bestowed to her by others, or to one another, Gladys avoided all temptation of boastful arrogance. Triumph over negative ideas and human self-centeredness worked wonders as she applied the positive energies being multiplied through serving to fill the needs of others. Assuming grace, there was no pretense in the image she portrayed. Preening requires precious time that detracts attention from focus on service to others, so, Gladys never indulged in weighing the value of her own nature. She was as unconscious of her virtue as Edgar Cayce was of his words when in trance.

Pooling the recorded transcriptions of Cayce's Readings, each with pertinent data of time, events and participants involved, was followed by updated accounts of case histories resulting from applications of prescribed directions. She awarded researchers with unlimited fruits of her dedication to their joint mission that mankind's enlightenment be assured. Through sharing an understanding of potential progress for each prodigal soul in mapping its return to the spiritual home of our Creator, Gladys thus dedicated her life in service for all of us as beneficiaries. What a legacy from the spirit meant to be known as Gladness!

Generations following their path on this foundation are the beneficiaries of the efforts of Edgar and Gladys through the eras of Egypt, Persia, Palestine and twentieth century America. Over and over the lessons of history trace their efforts to re-establish an awareness of our spiritual source for Earth's reincarnated souls since their entry as physical inhabitants. From their Atlantean assignment through challenges of diverse roles, their bonds of spiritual affinity have remained intact.

I used to introduce Gladys to new acquaintances as "Gladys, the Glue." One day she finally asked, "Micki, do you see me as the old horse ready for the glue factory?"

"Oh no, Gladys, you're the glue that holds us all together, Love Itself." Love personified, humility in perpetual service. I was amazed that she could not realize herself as the treasure that was so obvious to all of us who saw her as an embodied angel among her fans. She was accustomed to a concept of service, minus the accolades that honor her contributions to the cause, sensing team role, crediting others as leaders.

On one occasion, a new member was very impressed as she heard an account of how Mr. Cayce had prepared himself for the ritual of setting aside his conscious mind to enter the state of receptive attunement. Then, on cues observed by Mrs. Cayce as readiness for the questions, she began to pose them on behalf of the seeker's quest. He gave the answers as Gladys recorded it all on her steno-pad. When her notes were duly transcribed and typed, with a specified number of carbon copies, Gladys distributed them for use, retaining one copy for their permanent files.

"Oh, wouldn't it have been wonderful if today's technology could have been available? With a voice recorder taping we could all hear them played for the world's audience!" she enthused. Videotapes were not yet in common use at the time of her comment.

Gladys seemed stunned by the idea. "Oh, Honey, then I would have been out of a job!" That was the only time I ever heard her express a concern of self-interest. But then, she was no ordinary scribe.

Micki, Gladys and Mildred Davis

Selfless Devotion

Her secretarial skills were a necessity, of course, but her "job" entailed a myriad catalogue of duties that she incorporated as service to the Work, while sharing the chores of the Cayce family care as a number one commitment. Keeping the home open for the constant flow of people who sought comfort and the friendship of each member of their household, plus the Readings when given there, prayer and study group members, media researchers and journalists required a master juggler of coordination.

Then the community with its schools, churches, friends and those who served as operators, owners, managers and staff of local establishments required time and diplomatic exchange of her concerns as well. Always gracious in social encounters or business dealings, she helped establish rapport between the community and the family, while Cayce's talents were viewed in awe as strange by the local residents. Closeness was warily marginalized as they struggled to find a respectable niche. Activity within the church, especially as Mr. Cayce became a regular teacher of a Sunday school class, aroused interest of some whose friendships flourished to enhance their residency at Virginia Beach.

As Gladys grew in grace and maturity, she placed great emphasis on her personal Readings, while advice given to others inspired her to further develop her own spiritual potential. Half of her salary continued to be generously applied to sustaining her younger siblings and her mother, while a fourth of it was given to Mrs. Cayce for room and board. So practicality and responsibility were innate qualities that meshed well with her sensitive attitude of "Gladitude." Service to others involved her attention so fully that the least compliment or gift to her was a welcome surprise.

I found it interesting that Morton Blumenthal, on whose financial support the Cayces most depended for many years, was particularly aware of her selflessness. The rarity of expressions such as this for her, so encapsulates my own adoration of her generous nature that I want to repeat the attention I attributed earlier. Further details of his gift are added to underscore recognition of her special incorporated attributes.

Nicknaming her "Sunshine," he commended her with his expression of gratitude for her rare example. With a generous check of $300 dollars for her first Christmas at Virginia Beach in 1925, his letter read:

If ever service, sacrifice and devotion to a cause and ideal merited respect, merited joy, merited all the good wishes of Man, your giving of yourself to the psychic work, to the work of doing for others without thanks or any sign of physical appreciation in return, yours does. I am sure Edgar and the family agree with me in this, but that which I mean to convey is my personal appreciation for your work and my heart-felt thanks to the fine and noble contribution you have given and to the benefit they have brought into my life and the life of those dear to me. You choose to remain in a small corner, giving your time and efforts to a work that you and I both know is the first in God's realm.

She treasured personal notes and gifts of appreciation for her services, as all of us do, but in her wholesome observations, she valued the merits expressed to others just as sincerely. Witnessing the resulting inspiration of appreciation voiced or written to Mr. Cayce through the years, she mourned their lack when breaches in relationships altered their communication. Years later, after attending Morton's funeral she answered a query concerning his estranged relationship with A.R.E.'s members: "I believe he suffered the lack of appreciation, or hearing it expressed for his service in our behalf." If anyone could understand that omission, she had ample experience, though she had mastered its challenge early in her youth.

Gladys was aware that her mission in life was with sharing the wisdom of God through Edgar Cayce's Readings from her first day on the job as his secretary. Leaving her parents, siblings and friends to move with the Cayce family as the position required held no regrets, however. Granted, she faced loneliness and the ordinary yearnings that all youths endure when their social contacts are sparse. As the eldest child, she felt a great responsibility to help her parents and younger siblings during those lean financial years. Being exceptionally frugal in spending for her own self-gratification, she generally shared her meager salary with no obvious winces of sacrifice. "Others" was her mantra, innately chosen. If for no other reason, she merited sainthood by foregoing the normal amenities of life.

During a period of membership expansion that allowed for raises in salary, she was elated to reap the benefits that she deemed wealthy. Her salary was $12,000 per year. (So was Mae G. St. Clair's.) When a drop in the economy called for reduction in A.R.E.'s expenses, Hugh Lynn informed her that they would have to reduce staff expenses by sizeable cut-backs, he would be putting many on reduced hours. Mae would be limited to $4,000. She protested that Mae would not be able to survive on such a meager amount. He insisted that the cut was necessary. She made a deal with him to cut her own salary to $8,000 and give Mae $8,000. I believe that Mae never knew that, and I often felt tempted to enlighten her about "which side her bread was buttered on," as we use the term.

Gladys had a remarkable capacity to focus on each individual in a manner that expressed undivided attention with an affection that elevated their own sense of worth. Feeling good within her own aura inspired hope in improving others' potential. She had so perfected the target of her vision to view only one's potential goodness that her greeting met one's sense of absolution. Gravity lost its hold on self-awareness when one's response rose to meet her approval. It was like the magic of levitation for the spirit of her associates. Even recalling such memories renews their essence of rejuvenation.

To a great extent, each pioneer of this A.R.E. mission has been a blessing in expressing their individual magnetism of spiritual progress. Their sincere enthusiasm has been contagious while they worked to keep the precepts alive in their dealings and the philosophical lessons applied. Our lives have been enriched through connection with any link in the chain.

I recall that as children we would hold hands to form a human chain. Using an electric generator of low voltage, one touched a charged, bare wire, and its current passed through each body along the line. The mild shock was a stimulant of giggles, to say the least. Giggles may not be contagious among these more serious adults but their Joy is irresistible. Gladness, charged by her innate spiritual awareness, can still be serving smiles through the masses that are touched by the fruits of her Work. I am kept aware of it from each contact with the "live wires" involved.

The "Work"

When Gladys referred to "the Work," she meant the continued commitment of a mission that had been assigned to a group of kindred souls.

Eons ago, she and her twin soul, Edgar Cayce, were chosen to lead this tribe of entities in maintaining a special school of "Lifeguards." That is my nickname for today's group, since the headquarters for this era is set beside the Atlantic Ocean. At Virginia Beach, Virginia, the Association for Research and Enlightenment sits as an imposing structure on a hillside facing its eastern waterfront. It acts as a Lighthouse for diverse and sundry souls. Its beacon "Welcomes" all seekers.

From Atlantis, where they began their Earth mission, Gladys and Edgar Cayce have incarnated many times. Through lifetimes in Egypt, Persia, France, Israel and America, they have invariably magnetized their group of like-minded souls to join them in renewing their dedicated efforts. During each venture, the teamwork of enlightenment nurtured the educational benefits of physical, mental, emotional and spiritual attunement. Balance in serving Providence is the Master Key of their lessons to mankind, mentally, physically, socially and spiritually.

"The Work" still continues to inspire the world. An insatiable appetite exists for the reservoir of information gleaned from Akashic Records which Edgar Cayce translated during his Readings. As an avid Bible advocate, dedicated to its influence and the application of its guidance, his charted course bore the fruits of spiritual attunement. The unlimited reach of his psyche, or soul knowledge, served God's purpose in awakening that connection from within his fellow men and women as seekers of Truth.

Professing no exclusive gift other than that as given to every entity born into the world, he encouraged all souls to "Search for God" through their innate individual link of eternal life. Crediting spiritual leaders throughout history who had espoused that theory of our natural heritage, his adoration of Jesus' "Christ Consciousness as Comforter" was genuinely instructive.

Edgar Cayce traced the connection of Jesus as the first "begotten" son of our Creator to Alpha/Omega. When the morning stars sang together, the music of the spheres vibrated as a universal force of eternal LIFE. So when Jesus, in the role model of His parable of the Prodigal Son, having desired to use free will to set up a kingdom of self control, soon realized its failure. Separated from the Presence of Love, Light and Life's renewable source of its generation, He returned to a welcome of forgiveness for selfish ambition. Offering Himself to shepherd those followers who had been led astray and stranded in their wanderings, God allowed Him the opportunity to shepherd

the lost lambs. Through many lifetime paths of spiritual leadership, the ultimate self-sacrifice was executed when, as Jesus, He allowed His crucifixion and death. In sacrificing self for others' sake, in obedience to God, His Resurrection was the result of glorifying the Creator's Spirit as the bond of Love that unites All Life Force.

Choosing to follow the guidelines set by Him as the ideal Pattern promises the Feast of a Prodigal's Return to all who are willing to participate. Through the Christ Consciousness link, we can receive His help if we seek it. My conclusion in understanding may differ from scholars worldwide. The beauty of God's Free Will is in the individuality of choice of ideals and beliefs from which we can learn to grow.

Through the Edgar Cayce Readings came a history of our universe, often verifying or paralleling scientific theories, frequently surpassing that known at the time he expressed them. Identifying that about 13-14 billion years ago our universe began in a cosmos even older, existing before the Big-Bang-Birth, might inspire an appreciation of the Eternal Source of spirit, mind and body. Not that I presume to understand its verity, but the awe in wondering its significance is irresistible. Relativity in his shared information invites an evaluation of the reason for creation of souls, whether as participants, or mere observers.

Cayce's Readings extend awareness of life as a gift to its responsibility of cooperation with its Provider. Understanding the motive of Love's generosity inspires appreciation, or what I call "Gladitude." "One-der-full" use of its potential translates that the knowledge of Oneness into wisdom.

Within the body of information given for individuals, there are references of existence when their spirits experienced projection into matter before Atlantis. Cayce described Atlantis as the "first Eden" when Amilius led a group of spiritual beings as they began the "human experiment."

References to soul travel through many spheres and eons of time was a means of for individuals to learn service through centering spiritual chakras in cooperation with Nature. Moving through the birth/death/rebirth of reincarnation sheds light on the purification processes involved. Working on principles of growth in the educational steps of attitudinal healing through forgiveness brings greater tolerance and harmony. Errors of omission and commission are treated with expert counsel.

Privileged to study the archived collection of divinely inspired material in the Edgar Cayce Readings, I am grateful to so many dedicated souls who have made greater access to the Readings possible for seekers.

Field of Philosophical Reflections

Having grown up on a large farm as a microcosm of introduction to the World that I have experienced, I still relate to the expressions as reference guides for evaluation. Domestic aides assisted my mother in tending the needs of household activities of the health and social care of the menagerie of adults, children, garden and animals. My Dad's lumber business employed a variety of workers with specialized skills, most of whom were heads of families who lived on our farm. Their family members worked in the fields that produced fruits, vegetables, grains, nuts and cotton. Sharing the work load and the fruits of all their labors bonded our community as a family. Individual concerns were allied in the pool of interdependency. Isolation was impossible, as was privacy, in such a conglomeration of humanity.

So, when I use terms such as "field hands," I refer to the services of those who have the interests of the beneficiaries of their labors. Whether in the field of Education, Science, Health Care, Politics or Religion, the diversity of approach varied as much as the crop productions of our family farm.

No field of interest surpasses that of the spiritual impact that Religion plays in the cultures of people. Belief and Faith, with their wide array of interpretive views or creeds, can trigger altercations of passions which defy reasonable discussion or civil dialogue. Religion can become a minefield of communication, wherein most of the world's battles have erupted into full blown wars between nations and regional cultures. Our identities, though individually wrapped, are tied in bundles of associations. Each bundle is a magnet for like-minded souls with varying degrees of power for the good or destructive evolution of society.

Wise use of our intellectual capacities is required to examine our options in choosing our association within Religious Belief Systems. As cautious as parents choosing their child's custodial care while they work away from home, entrusting our spiritual application to the rules, evaluations or guidelines of any group requires careful consideration. Since our attitude sets the direction of life's course, it is imperative we choose friends who boost our spirits in the way we wish to fulfill our potential, none more pertinent than in sharing our spiritual identity. In first knowing ourselves, we recognize compatible or incompatible traits in others.

Edgar Cayce encouraged others to pursue their Church or Synagogue affiliations as they grew in understanding God's plan for their participation. Although he identified his own belief in attending a Christian Protestant church where he regularly taught a Bible Study class, the Readings made no negative dispersions of other belief systems. As long as God was worshiped as their source of life, their emphasis focused on each entity's link within as awareness for guidance.

Membership of A.R.E. has never excluded seekers of any denomination, though some individual members may have preferred that their biased views control the limits of other's rights to participate. Zealots of such self-righteousness seem to abound throughout recorded history. The late twentieth century breed of them seem no less obnoxious than some "Crusaders" might have been if disarmed of their swords. Cycles of domineering "Christians" attempt to "wall-out" even other Christians with whom they may disagree.

Our American Founders faced this dilemma in trying to allow all of God's children to share a state of freedom from the tyranny of such religious tyrants. Even after 234 years of a secular Democracy, many fail to appreciate the separation of Church and State in governing our citizens. Ecumenical worship, according to our evolving soul development allows us to harmonize our mutual oneness as human/divine siblings. Too few organizations survive with such a warm open welcome for Research and Enlightenment and its liberal application.

Scales of values are not standardized, though digitalized in finger pointing, perhaps. The prominent digit, the index Jupitarian pointer, directs obedience while the Saturn digit, when the "director" fails, is universally applied. Contemplative thought is rare, it seems, when leaders disagree. Edgar Cayce emphasized that thoughts are "things," changeable, rearrange-able as tools of the mind. "Mind is the builder" is the mantra. Sound judgment should perform as the mind's architect although seldom is it evident, especially in politics.

The field hands of this group helped Edgar Cayce establish their community of souls who sought to have him guide their flock. Committed to the personal application of prayer and Bible study, he continued Readings sought for health needs among them. Leaders were groomed to lecture, and healthcare therapists trained by experts, such as Dr. Harold J. Reilly, an Osteopath, that Cayce had sent patients before his "shingle" was hung. Dr. Reilly, like many physicians whom the Readings directed individuals to seek for their necessary care, had no prior awareness of Edgar Cayce before the patient arrived. Fascinated by the "psychic instructions" as being so ideally correct, he made the effort to get better acquainted, as did many others. Establishing their immediate rapport, their friendships bridged the eons with mutual respect and continuity. His commitment to the A.R.E. was dedicated to training therapists for a clinic that was added to the old Hospital Building when, in 1956, it was revived as Headquarters, long after Mr. Cayce had died.

The Reilly School of Massotherapy is still a part of A.R.E., along with the Atlantic University which began before the Cayce Hospital was closed during the Great Depression of the Thirties. Again, we owe thanks to such devoted members whose generosity paid fees to keep its accreditation alive through the "lean years;" Dr. Brown, Robert Adriance and William Lord, now all gone but not forgotten. They left big footprints.

Generous donors included those who had Readings for family, friends and concerns of history that answer questions for those of us who study their recorded answers today. Donations by members of the Search For God groups whose "meager financial contributions" have been a vital aspect of A.R.E.'s survival, help keep the organization alive and growing for the benefit of generations to come with the addition of our Library Building and the Visitor Center. As passionate as Gladys was during times of economic stress for Edgar Cayce and the Work, I am sure that all those who pioneered this spiritual vineyard share her concern during our present challenges in support of the Work.

Reincarnation

In a world that dates its age in millions of years, we call our present time capsule the twenty-first century. Being thus afflicted with short term memory, "Eternity" is no longer comprehensible. Although we like to think we can relate to that period of time when the morning stars sang in harmonic vibrations, as the universes were initially being created, finding an explanation as to why we think that is a challenge. So I will not try to open that doorway. If I ever had its key, it was long ago misplaced.

Closed to our religious consciousness for so long, reincarnation has been resurrected through chaotic responses. Global travel and technological advances in communication have so fused the dialogue of Theological students and scholars since my college days. Resurfacing to reawaken our soul memories, or at least to add credence to our toddlers' dreams and visions of past lives before their cultural deletion, discussions of such possibilities are breaking through the walls of disbelief. Orthodox churches are slow to let down their barriers which have for so long given them power over their congregations of unaware sheep. Their challenge is impeded by confrontations for which they have no armor of its essential Truth or training.

A few decades will be necessary to bridge the faith gaps that follow as the masses hold on to the frayed rope of disbelief. Theodora's crime of pandemic consequences will be diagnosed as a plague for many fragile faiths. Victims of her self-righteous delusions were implanted with its antidote of honesty, which can be activated if the art of humility can be located. Let us hope that, in this period of history when the plagues of prophetic challenges seem more imminently foreboding than ever before, we can be prepared to face our necessary transitions of body, mind and spirit.

According to the Readings, Gladys Davis and Edgar Cayce had been introduced to the scene even before God had designed the physical clay model for Adam's incarnation, but waited their turns in the spiritual realm until their assignments were duly processed for entering on the World's stage.

The Edgar Cayce Readings answered the requests of thousands of individuals who sought his intercessory skills which brought messages of hope in treating their frail bodies, minds and spirits. They form a foundation for study in the Archives of A.R.E. Gladys Davis, with the help of Mr. Cayce's sons, Hugh Lynn and Edgar Evans, used her preserved copies of the

Readings as they were expressed through him while he lay in a meditative trance state. Now that they have been converted to digital media for Internet usage, the legacy of the Work is available to seekers, students and scholars around the world.

Within a library of books and articles already available are the details of their history of survival and the process of establishing an International Headquarters in Virginia Beach through the challenges of difficult economic and emotional stresses. Some powerful individuals have assisted in promoting the organization, many of whom I have been privileged to know.

As one of the millions of its beneficiaries, I am grateful to all supporters of the joint mission that Edgar Cayce and Gladys Davis undertook in our behalf. My gratitude extends past the present members who lead and carry on the Work of Research and Enlightenment, through the generations that will be inspired to continue it. From all cultures, religions or philosophies, humankind shares its roots in mutual divinity, where Love is the glue of Harmony, and Peace, throughout the Universe of Its Creation. In wholeness we share Enlightenment of our humanity's divine nature.

Those who heard of Edgar Cayce's unique diagnostic ability sought in desperation his intercession with God. Stories scattered across the nation as newsworthy events because of his strange mode of operandi. Through prayerful effort to set aside his conscious mind in auto-hypnotic meditation, he allowed questions that produced his vocal answers, informed as though the Almighty was the direct source of his edification. Used as "news scoops," the public's attention was assured, thus setting investigating hounds on his trail. Reticent by nature to cash in on a celebrity status, Cayce focused on the gift of God's grace, trying desperately to keep a balance with his ego.

The challenges of their lives were pressures that surpass the normal choices of humanity due to the attunement levels of spiritual awareness. Impossible to ignore was the path Cayce had chosen for his earthly life mission to continue the work that was prepared for him even before his becoming a man. "There are no accidents," as his understanding was well aware. Each family member was positioned in their specific roles at this stage of time and place. Gradually revealed to him through his interpretive study, using his own talent skills, he shared these insights with all who chose to participate in their revelations. Hugh Lynn often referred to his father as an

"Internal Astronaut," not wishing to be "a psychic" yet seeing all souls as being psychic in varying degrees of their own awareness or insight.

Equally unique, Gladys was qualified to share their joint mission for the twentieth century. For twenty-two years with the Cayce family as they assembled individuals and groups whose records we can now review, followed by over forty years where she persevered in ensuring the survival of the Readings, she assured their use verbatim, protected from alterations that may have diminished their original value. Her noble purpose was fulfilled with such grace that no witness remains that can identify her sweat. Her selfless service looked so easy to all of us who knew her intimately. Compassion for the frailties of others as identified in lives of the saints, achieving such status while overcoming adversity, leaves us with no doubt of her mastery of that echelon. Her legacy of accomplishments in our behalf is due our salute!

Over the period of half a century, Edgar Cayce uttered more than fourteen million words while in an unconscious state, words which tell of the creation of the universe and the role of Earth's inhabitants, past, present and future. Countless books, articles, lectures, studies and discussions have centered on the messages he expressed as he lay in that self-induced trance-like state, thanks to the preservation of the Readings.

When radio waves were harnessed and their broadcasts permeated the sound barriers from the horn of a cabinet-box, the world's attention was hypnotized by its magic. Communication of the vocal messages transformed the planet. As remote as the declarations of John the Baptist from the wilderness of Palestinian hills, the quiet native of Kentucky projected the messages of God with the words of the Readings to the amazement of all who listened and applied their tenants.

Reflecting Readings

One of many of Mr. Cayce's admirers among physicians was inspired by witnessing the phenomena of uncanny expertise in diagnostic perception and the range of therapy recommended as ideal treatments for potential improvements, even cures, when medical science at the time presented no clues as to cause and effect. He expressed his approval in many recommendations to friends, family and patients that they seek his psychic insight as an adjunct health and life enhancement benefit.

Explaining that Mr. Cayce was a modest and honorable man who made no claim of medical knowledge, requested recipients of his Readings have their physicians check and compare their customary exams and methods in validating any diagnosis given. M.L. Richardson, D.O., further summarized Edgar Cayce's *mode of operandi* in the Report for Reading 514-1:

> Mr. Cayce is a psychic who goes into a trance, or a self-imposed hypnosis. While in that state, he is consulted on the matters of the research quest, whether health or other concerns. His wife and stenographer are present, conducting and recording the consultation. Most of those who seek his counsel, he has never seen, nor is there a description given him, and they need not be present during his Reading. A copy is provided of the words he speaks, verbatim, including answers to questions that follow his discourse of condition, cause and cure, and prescriptions with precise and pertinent definitive information.

As requests broadened from health to philosophical concerns, including reincarnation, or religious and historical information, they explored the gamut of man's search for knowledge and understanding. Probing prehistoric records, long deleted from memory of humanity's awareness, the Readings' insight often replaced a two-dimensional black and white concept with a full-scale Technocolor 3-D movie rendition of an event. They turned once barely surmised suppositions into plausible explanations of contemplative wonder.

Readings from Atlantean or Lemurian entrance of souls, through Egyptian, Mongolian, Persian, Palestinian, Roman and Early American (North and South) lifetimes were given. With the many re-encounters of individual relationships, Edgar Cayce quilts the patterns together in stitching Earth's history through the harmony and chaos of major events. In fact, the geographical map of the planet was not the limit of soul-travel, as some Readings detailed intermissions of interplanetary studies and activities influencing soul evolvement.

Souls drawn into his sphere of commitment were magnetized by his ideal: to make manifest man's relationship to his Maker and man's relationship to his fellow man. Entering Earth during a very chaotic period of history, their willingness to endure its challenges have always benefited others, inspiring them to better apply God's spiritual heritage. Their prophetic view of the changes that earthlings face today is apropos in preparation for potential shifts in polar magnetism, whether mental or physical adjustments, which require greater awareness of our common bond in enlightened Oneness. Our allegiance to God assures that we exhibit Love in helping one another. Today's survival situations demand it.

One of the best examples that I have seen during this lifetime of using one's full potential in service to humanity is a wonderful mutual friend of Gladys. An active leader in the use of the Cayce healing techniques, Dr. Gladys McGarey represents the top echelon of medical professionals in our world, of which I have had ample access during the past century. She and a fellow A.R.E. member, Dr. C. Norman Shealy, have headed a team of enlightened souls whose expertise established the basis for an additional Institute of Health in Bethesda, Maryland, for Alternative Medicine, along with their many gifts of healing aids in physical, mental and spiritual attunement. I have known both of them as exemplary souls for many years; my gratitude for their services to humanity has no bounds. To be able to share her contribution for this book of treasured memories of our beloved friend, I am overjoyed.

Dr. Gladys Taylor McGarey reflects:

> I knew and loved Gladys in this life time from 1956 until she died. And I still love and miss her. My initial contact with her was when we first wrote to the A.R.E., and she answered our letter in a simple gracious response.
>
> After that, every year when we went back to the Beach we spent wonderful hours with her. We talked about philosophy, questions we had from the Readings and shared dreams we had about the future of A.R.E. Through the years whenever we had a question about some medical concept in a Reading she was always the one we went to for clarification and help. And she always was able to help. The work with the medical aspects of the Readings never would have gone anywhere without her. As a spin-off from that, the A.R.E. Clinic, the American Holistic Medical Association and a host of other organizations which needed her work to become the transformative movement they are today.

When we started the A.R.E. Clinic she was a founding board member and the secretary of the board. She kept us on track for years. I remember going out to the Casa Grande property when we first received it. Just walking the desert land with her as she talked about when Edgar had come out here and she had pictures of him in that desert, she said it was like the "City of The Hills and Plains" which the Readings talked about.

At lunch time that day she drew on a napkin her dream of an integrated healing center where many different disciplines would work together recreating the healing center of ancient times. This was probably about 1971 when M.D.s and D.O.s were not able to work together, and the idea of an integrated center was truly only a dream.

Now her dream is a reality in many places going far beyond the Arizona desert. She quietly and lovingly influenced my life and really changed the course of modem medicine helping it recognize its spiritual mission. What a blessing she was to all of humanity.

Dr. McGarey and other dedicated professionals with similar sensitivities have incorporated the tenets necessary to expand use of holistic healing worldwide. Born of missionary parents to India, her expertise in gynecology and obstetrics has inspired emphasis on life's values in planning families with functional eternal qualities. Her book, *"The Physician Within,"* is one that I highly recommend to everyone.

Another healer among A.R.E.'s fabulous members for so many years added this next shared comment through my granddaughter, Alexis. Her excerpt resulted from a recorded telephone conversation with Helen Ruth Schroeder, then 83 years old, on January 29, 2008. Helen helped start the A.R.E. conferences at Asilomar in California. Her comments are:

"I learned about the A.R.E. [when I was living] in Texas, when Bridey Murphy was on the best seller list, way before your time! We read the book and were fascinated by it and we wrote to Virginia Beach for more to read. Then we went to hear Gina Cerminara, and we heard about the study group, Van and Hazel Gregory's group. That was in 1957. I learned massage later in California. My husband changed his work in 1959, and we went to California. I was in a study group and met Dawn Aheart, an RN who got her Ph.D., went to Phoenix and learned the Cayce-Reilly massage from the A.R.E. Clinic there. Then she came back to California, where she lived, and taught it to those of us who wanted to learn."

"When did you first meet Gladys?" Alexis asked.

"Bless her pea-pickin' heart," Helen Ruth began. "It was my first trip to Virginia Beach, and I was really green at the time, especially on metaphysics. But I was raised Catholic, and Catholics believed in miracles, so that really opened doors for me, ironically enough. It formed a stability for my early life. I was still very new, and I joined what was then called a project group. At that time, summer school at the A.R.E. was two weeks long, during which they would provide the opportunity for anybody and everybody to join what they called a project group. It was very similar to a study group in some ways. We ate together, we worked together, we lived together in dormitories. It was a very enriching experience."

"We were told to keep a journal and to keep track of our dreams. I didn't remember my dreams—that was not something I'd been aware of or thought about before. So they told us to put a pad of paper and a pencil by our bed. As we went to sleep, we were supposed to say to ourselves, 'I will remember my dreams.' I didn't have very much confidence in that, but I tried it anyway. The next morning, sure enough, I did not remember my dreams. So the following night, I said, 'I want to remember my dreams,' because I could believe in that, and doggone it if it didn't make the difference! I did remember a dream in the morning!"

"I dreamed I saw an open loose-leaf notebook, and the format of the page was the format of a Cayce Reading as you read it in the library."

"Now I didn't really see anything but a number in the upper right hand corner, which is the way they start, and I just knew it was an Edgar Cayce Reading. So I dashed down to the library, and it was not in the library yet, and the reason it wasn't in the library yet. That was because Gladys was still deleting names and replacing them with numbers. So, I talked to Ruth Lenoir, who was a librarian at that point, and she said to go ask Gladys."

"So Gladys, God love her, had her office in the basement of the old Hospital Building at the time. I didn't talk to her at the time, but I told someone at the office my story, and they passed it on to Gladys. She was inundated with work, God bless her, but Gladys looked the Reading up for me, and she wrote a memo to me, giving the gist of the Reading content by that number. It was talking about a child, as I remember it, who had a blood condition and died of a blood condition, and that was the information. However, I think the reason I had that dream was that in 1953 I had had a little baby girl. My first child was a boy, and my second child was a little baby girl."

"She was just fine when she was born, but at the age of two years, she had what they diagnosed as sinus thrombosis, which is like a blood clot in one of the veins of the head. I woke up one morning and the baby was limp, so I called the doctor immediately, and that's when they did what was called an air study. She was in shock at the time, and their diagnosis was that it had affected the entire circuits of her brain. So she recovered from that, in that she survived it, but she was in a vegetative for the rest of her life—for seven years."

"And so this dream, I think, in '59 (and she was born in 1953), was telling me to not expect or struggle or worry about her survival, that she was okay, but that she would not get well again. When we moved to California, I was advised by a psychologist that she be put in a facility that would care for her. So we did, when the boy was three, and it was air-conditioned—and this was in Texas, so that counts for a lot. When we moved, she remained in the hospital, and I would visit periodically. And again, it was air-conditioned, and you have no idea how much that counts in Texas."

"I learned about the Readings in the interim. I was puzzling over whether I should bring her home now, because I wasn't sure that the psychologist had given me the right advice. Then, I had a meditation experience the second time I was at the Beach in which I saw her standing like a little girl, blonde hair, big dress, just standing there. So that's where the dream about the notebook came back, and I came out of meditation with the knowing that I was to bring her home."

"So when I got back to California and I talked to my husband about it, he was reluctant mainly because he thought it would be a strain on me. And I said, 'Well, that's what I'd like to do. It took me seven years to figure this out, so you take as long as you want.' He took a couple of months."

"So I called this little clinic where she was staying, and they were very reluctant to take her out because she couldn't even eat by herself. I couldn't find any place that would teach me how to tube feed her."

"By then, through reading the Cayce Readings, I had become aware that there was consciousness, a soul inside that I could communicate with. So my husband was making a business trip to Dallas, and we arranged for Jan (that was her name) to come back with him to California. I had found a reasonably close facility where I could visit her often."

"I would go in and I would talk to her. So I think the purpose of the whole thing, really did get served, because she actually died just a number of months later. It was Thanksgiving and my husband's parents were visiting with us at the time. My husband had really been able to bond with her, and I think it took me just as long to learn my lesson as it took Jan to grow spiritually for whatever she was here for."

"All of this had a level of cooperation on my part, rather than resistance and struggling, because of that dream that I had. Because Gladys was so sweet and so kind to take time out to take care of my dream. She always had her arms open to welcome everybody. That was the welcoming thing that endeared me to A.R.E. She contributed to my well-being at every level. She came out to California to visit the groups out in California, and when she was there I had the good fortune of having her stay at my home. There are two things that stay in my mind about that visit."

"My son who did not keep his room very clean, didn't get his room clean in time for Gladys to arrive. He took everything out of his room and put it in the hallway. And then Gladys arrived and had to climb over it, which she did with grace and humor."

"By then, I had been a regional representative for A.R.E. and was into starting new study groups. When I started, that chapter on meditation was a total mystery to me. I couldn't identify with the language in it. I was concerned about starting with the meditation chapter. For people who know nothing about meditation in any form, they might have a degree of difficulty with it. Another thing is, if you had a background in, say, TM, meditation to them would mean one thing and it's not the same thing as in the Readings."

"So I was unsure about starting a new study group with meditation. I felt we could start with cooperation as Group #1 did, and later on down the line, after ideals, you could work in meditation. So I discussed that with Gladys, and I asked her what they did about it in the very beginning."

"She said, of course the affirmation at the beginning of each chapter was given just for that—to meditate on, to be the desire you hold in meditation, and we just did it any way we could, and there's a Reading that says that if you just do that enough, you will eventually just HAVE it. Frequently it was just prayer and not meditation. So, when starting new groups, we started with cooperation. And by then, the A.R.E. meditation course became available, so we were able to offer that to our study group."

"What is your fondest memory of Gladys?" Alexis asked.

"The time that she spent in my home, because I had more time with her. Other times, I tried to be aware of how busy she was and how many demands there were on her time. So we would have a meal or something like when I went to Virginia Beach. But she would share—I remember going to one of those mid-afternoon free lectures and I remember her sharing then some of her stories. One thing I remember is that someone in the audience must have brought the subject up, so she told them about a Reading to her or a dream, that fennel was good for gas."

"But she was always, I think the strongest memory I have of her was her friendliness, her openness, her sharing, just open arms ready to hug anyone. I haven't been active in a while, but in earlier years Hugh Lynn asked me to start the camp program at Asilomar. In the very beginning it was for adults only. I remember, I had two boys by then and, when I went to Asilomar by myself, I thought how great it would be to bring my boys up there. Hugh Lynn finally asked me if I would start the children's camp in 1963, and I said, 'Yes,' not knowing what I was getting into."

"I did that for a couple of years, and then Nancy Richardson took over when I went to Pennsylvania to be with my mother for a little while. So when she returned she started doing classes for adults. In the interim I had had an ongoing study group for children, with an age range from 5 to 11. It was great!"

Helen Ruth was a devoted healing channel who, at 85, died in Phoenix, Arizona. She and I were in close communication as she faced her transition with a peaceful approach in anticipating her soul's gift in further enlightenment and harmony. Her sons can follow with pride.

Among the contributions that benefits A.R.E. are researchers that study and apply the Readings for causes that inspire improvements in healing body, mind and soul. Writers, teachers, archeologists, scientists and staff have spread the messages that awakened the public to participation. Gladys assisted so many in locating avenues to speed their progress. Professor Fran Moreau of Miami shared a story of her coming into the Library one afternoon to invite him and others to attend a viewing of the Crystal Skull, as its owner shared her story of finding it in South America when a child. That instigated an interest that has set him on a path of interest which still intrigues him as he pursues involvement. He has been a great help to me in sharing our ongoing friendship with many others.

Mark Finnan, a Canadian playwright and film maker, remembered her fondly as he interviewed her years ago while studying about the Master and the Essenes. Sharing his taped interview with her, I saw another sample of her open praise of Edgar Cayce's expertise as seer, an exemplary soul with a "regular fellow" ego, as friend and teacher.

Linda Keener appreciated Gladys' willingness to join the conferees as they gathered groups for photos recording their visits, adding to their treasured memories of special friends.

Ellie Eshelman, an avid researcher of the Readings, was one of the most diversified helpers ever, who gave her expertise in promoting the passions of others from the Meridian Group researching health alternatives to ancient sites of treasures, relics, social and religious symbology. Typing, editing, researching as an aide for staff members or greeting visitors at the front desk, her lovely disposition expanded in service wherever needed. I was often so blessed. Her note states:

> Now, I really didn't know Gladys, other than to say hello when she passed by while I worked at the front desk. Most striking about her was her wonderful smile, not just from her lips, but also from her eyes. I did know her on a different level, though, as the silent partner in the Readings. It was from those Readings that I came to admire her patient work behind the scenes, taking shorthand, typing up the Readings, and answering correspondence. Never in the spotlight, ever present, though, through the years on the pages of the Readings. To paraphrase the old adage: never have so few done so much—Gladys, Gertrude, and Edgar—three people who gave of themselves to bring us the Readings. Gladys was the momentum and the force that kept the Readings flowing.
>
> Several months before she passed away, I was at the front desk when she came down the staircase and over to the desk. As she spoke to me I understood that she was saying goodbye, not by her words, but more by a feeling of someone taking leave. I also sensed Mr. Cayce's presence standing beside her. I silently understood that she would be going to the other side before long. We exchanged small talk and pleasantries, but a same time, the heart of the inner dialogue was a gracious and genuine goodbye. Her work here was finished.

Edgar Cayce's devotion to Bible study strengthened his innate psychic and intuitive nature to keep him focused on his ability to teach others how to attune their own wills to recognize the value of spiritual alignment. Within the individual Readings of each soul history (Akashic Record) he translated meanings to awaken them to the choices they faced. Through his lectures to various groups, his many letters and written articles were mercifully saved by his devoted mission partner, so that from their sampling, many others can find comparable inspiration.

In one such letter, Edgar Cayce shared an interesting observation. Having recently given a reading for a Priest, then later, one for a Rabbi, residents of different areas, one in Montreal, Canada, the other in New York City, he was impressed that their replies arrived about the same time using identical words: "One realizes when reading the message from you, God again speaks to man through man." In his summary of their evaluations he commented, "Quite interesting, isn't it, when we consider how far apart we ordinarily feel these are in religious thought, yet with such expressions one finds they are not apart at all in their deeper thought."

Can there be any wonder that in listening to Edgar Cayce as he expressed the words of guidance to each Reading recipient, Gladys likewise attuned herself in harmony to their spiritual depths? Her response to the messages she recorded was implanted in her mind and heart as she translated, read and re-read each copy with the serious responsibility of sharing his commit-ment of service to their mutual Cause. Serving God and their fellow men, women, and children was their chosen occupation, for which they were ideally suited in complimentary roles.

My lifelong acceptance of reincarnation as a natural fact definitely sets me apart as a minority in the Western world, decades before its public awareness was being openly discussed. Hope dawns. For those of us born with past-life memory partially intact, the theory of reincarnation makes perfect sense in understanding the process of cause and effect, that events of history play in emotional response to trends in evolution, or devolution. For anyone deprived of the panoramic scope of soul evolution the perspective of reincarnations affords, it's no wonder that a rather myopic approach to relationships exists instead. God's Justice is veiled by ignorance of Universal Laws.

However, there are many parallels of insight I have found through long study and my gregarious openness in sharing ideas with others throughout my extended octogenarian lifetime. Since "like attracts like," or, "birds of a feather flock together," it is no wonder that my search for understanding has brought me the overflowing fountain of Edgar Cayce's pool of wisdom. Nor is it a mystery that Gladys Davis and I were drawn to a renewal of our many wonderful friendships in other places, with different names and faces, from times immemorial.

The Weaver of Life's skeins of spirit, time and matter has glorified Space with Her Art in patterns that repeat the appearance of our individual threads in random sequence. Never in boring repetition, She embroiders compositions of familiar textures in variable shapes and sizes. As seamless tapestries of the eons, whose unbroken threads weave memories that inspire Gladness with each successive re-encounter, we continue to interact with each other as we learn to use our true heritage of Divine Spirit.

It is fascinating that individuals return in families that share links with those who have ties to the same former lifetimes. For instance, the Blumenthal family, for whom Readings were given for numerous friends as well as their immediate kin. Morton's brother, Edwin, was the younger brother of Jesus, with an acquaintance who was formerly Judas Iscariot. Their father had been Jacob. As Jacob, then the father of twelve sons, Joseph being his favorite, having been the same entity that evolved later as Jesus. Within their group, connections with one another in different lifetimes kept a running series of their re-encounters. Within the Cayce family and the Davis clan, their members often were closely associated. Even if not by kinship, their paths shared parallel activities repeatedly.

Like the old movie serials of the *"Perils of Pauline,"* we seem to pick up the trails, or trials, left over from our last exit, carrying on the unfinished business. Sometimes, having done well, we are blessed to return to those with whom our bonds are so beneficial for harmonious progress. So, it seems the implication is to use each opportunity possible, to harmonize our relationships for the smoother terrain of future reunions.

Accounting Department

I fantasize by mentally picturing the Akashic Records. I envision them as physically invisible, intangible recordings spanning time and space which contain the entire karmic history of the evolution of humanity from the beginning of time. Or, I imagine them as being stacked in cavernous libraries, or tedious hand-painted scrolls of our initial years, until Time adapted to technological mass production with the digital speeds of today's computers.

Recycling old souls has its challenges, of course. If all creation occurred at one instance, what a bang it must have been! Has all the dust settled yet?

Is this the chaos out of which God is creating order of the cosmic universe? As evidence, our individuality sends out for consideration shoots of mental processing of variable knots. Tracing our embroidered threads requires concentrated focus. Some of us elders enjoy sorting our tangled knots of past links, if intuitive vision and patience permit. Occasionally, youngsters do, too. Maybe you have completed yours.

A soul dedicated to God's service for Earth's transients, Edgar Cayce came into this world well-equipped to help unravel such mysteries. Other helpers were drawn into the spiritual vortex to share the Work. Thank Goodness that Gladys Davis incarnated again to invest her complimentary talents in recording and preserving all those Readings, linking the material and spiritual worlds. Thus, we can continue to benefit from the dispensation of golden wisdom to be found by treasure seekers in the flakes of information gleaned from their sluices.

Edgar Cayce's Readings were requested by family members and friends whose health situations were severely encumbered with hopelessness, by suffering that had chronically failed to improve after medical efforts had exhausted signs of possible recovery. Medical facilities and physicians resigned hope of improvement, so as tales of Cayce's diagnostic successes spread, families sought his aid as a last resort. Tales of his weird method of lying on his back, praying himself to sleep and having someone pose questions for him to answer as he slept seemed so absurd. However, dire concerns often drive desperate people to grasp for seemingly desperate, last-ditch means before all hope is gone. The news of successive results for those who actually followed and applied the sage advice given by the unconscious man soon changed the tune from "weird" to the "Man of Miracles" as the number of seekers multiplied.

After years of giving almost exclusively Physical Health Readings, Edgar Cayce's Readings began explanations as to the underlying causes of ailments, including bits of information indicating conditions that originated in previous lifetimes. Being an avid Bible student and ardent Christian during the early twentieth century in America, Mr. Cayce found the concept of reincarnation preposterous, and in conflict with his former religious beliefs.

With his cautious nature and sincere desire to serve God in Truth, his devotion to prayerful scrutiny received overwhelming inner response in assurance that God was his Source of the records he was channeling to guide others. As he tested the Readings on his own Life Reading, then on close family and friends, a whole new world of material opened complete renovations of old concepts. Their spiritual devotion was enhanced as the horizon gradually expanded its vistas of broader, deeper reasoning ability, lifting veils from blind acceptance to clarifying understanding. His family harmonized in accepting its premise.

Each Life Reading with its variety of facets through events of history that shaped its viewpoints, or left its imprints during each process, inspires a study in psychology, philosophy, physiology and theology. Watching the kaleidoscopic formations of interactions in group patterns, like swirling flocks of birds on the wing reveal the bonds of their relationships even as they scatter or close their ranks, can lend a rainbow array of color to the stories handed down from ancient campfire gatherings.

When the character traits of personality described in a Reading shape events in harmony or discord, they are traced as repeating influences in ensuing incarnations of the soul. In later phases of history, we can see as souls reincarnate repeatedly how the lives of individuals make their imprint on factors that shape nations and their relationships with the world.

For instance, from the Cayce Readings, we learn that the soul known historically as Benjamin Franklin worked in a previous lifetime to bring harmony between the Egyptian people, their priests and the pharaohs. Helping set the rules governing immigrants and the indigenous Egyptians toward a prosperous era of cultural challenge, he etched their memories as future guides. Such past experience marked valuable boundaries for the wisdom he could impart among the coalition of individuals who eventually set the goals of America's Independence as a nation of freedom and justice for its citizens.

Fate used no fickle fingers in gathering the team of experienced statesmen to form the Union of United States of America. The Readings gave clues to many of Cayce's clients about their participation in both eras. In fact, the indexed files Gladys promoted for the A.R.E. list a large number of America's founders among them.

By exemplifying the role of diplomacy with European allies, Benjamin Franklin helped to bring victory for our independence, allowing our democracy to begin on the foundation of principles he and other associates had learned before the pyramids were built. His counterparts, also experienced in world affairs through former lifetimes, retained sub-conscious traces of soul memory to guide their insights. Sometimes that insight stemmed from lessons learned through success in former judgments, at other times from past failures.

Our country was established under the auspices of a most benevolent Creator whose control of the intricacies of reincarnation had gathered an array of souls whose mastery of wisdom in the arts of understanding human nature was exceptional. Franklin, Adams, Hamilton, Madison, Jefferson and the scores of fellow patriots assembled to act as our guides were well-founded in discipline and psychological reckoning. The "unalienable birthrights" of spiritual freedom were within their abilities to understand and respect. They knew, in establishing a foundation of laws, that principles of justice were basic. Respect through fairness inspired a cooperative community of patriots and set boundaries of ideal behaviors. Inherited circumstances and imperfect customs played havoc in their individual reasoning abilities. Yet, as a team, they excelled in consensus, choosing qualities of virtue for a system of government that surpassed the general status of nations of their era.

At times politicians give reason to ponder their potential past lives if, as history students, we see parallels of chaotic nations in decline, interspersed with later periods of enlightened development. If generational tribes have cycles of re-entry, one dares hope for healing in future rounds. Such reasoning inspires us to impart our ideals to our offspring and develop our own leadership potential for service as a means to ensure future periods of positive development.

Edgar Cayce's Readings encompass vivid histories describing the lives of numerous individuals whose influences shaped the destiny during our country's foundation. Before Cayce's death in 1945, some of our most prominent leaders, including President Franklin D. Roosevelt, were given guidance through special requests for information from the Source of the Readings.

It is awe-inspiring and somewhat mind-boggling to calculate the potential value and depth of an education gleaned from previous sojourns on this planet. We have access to these personal examples of constructive applications to create a far-reaching foundation, such as our Constitution, Bill of Rights and the Declaration of Independence, as well as many other inspiring guidelines. And, conversely, it is equally distressing to speculate that such valuable information and wisdom has been lost by Western civilization for so many generations, cowered by religious abuse of power, keeping the populace ignorant of our past lifetimes.

Nowadays, without awareness of prior incarnations as past training, since children have been discouraged to use recall mechanisms, the educational system is hampered from each start. Imagine writing messages on the wet seashore sands before the tide sweeps in. When incoming memories are allowed no contemplation before they are shushed, so much of their value is lost. From whence doth genius arise? Guessing is a tool of substitution, something used when more adequate tools are no longer available. Truth is often compromised by missing facts.

Cayce's ability to connect with, to read and translate Akashic Records for the few thousand souls who sought help, through Readings, for understanding their present ailments or predicaments and roots of their relationships, has provided our generation untold benefits in comprehension as we study the A.R.E. archives, thanks to their preservation by Gladys Davis.

Biblical Patches

Theology students, in particular, can now access information that fills in some of the many gaps in our Biblical history. The material given through Mr. Cayce was dependent on the seeker's request and was limited to his/her scope of desire, interest or applicability. Fortunately, there were a few individuals whose depth of understanding led them to compose questions that elicited extraordinary feedback, yielding greater insight for humanity as a whole. Would that more scholars might dare awaken their recognition intuitively!

A special boon for Biblical scholars is the fact that the Cayce Readings identified by name many individuals living in Judea during the time of Jesus and his followers. The maze of events and relationships from this period, as set forth in the Readings, is so complicated that few authors have managed to properly index the *Who's Who* list with any semblance of accuracy.

When Gladys and Hugh Lynn first began the sorting processes, everything had to be done by hand; technology in those days was still so very infantile that the methods required a "Methuselian" scholar to place each participant in her, or his, proper role on the genealogical chart. Their interconnections were so intertwined that even Einstein's Theory of Relativity would have proven useless as a tool.

For instance, as indicated by the Readings, the Essenes' Teacher of Righteousness led the Carmel group for a couple of hundred years as they awaited the promise of a Messiah. Preparations for His arrival included the choice of a very special birth-mother. Her preordained name would be "Mary." She would be honored among all women. The physical, mental and spiritual pedigrees of family and child would be studied seriously by Carmel's hierarchy of priests (both male and female), physiologists, astrologers and their wisest of teachers. As daughters were presented for evaluations, about a dozen would be accepted for training from the potential candidate's pool. For over 200 years, the Essenes, expecting the Messiah, prepared as they waited.

Readings given specifically for Tom Sugrue's book, *"There Is A River"* as well as those for the weekly prayer group, gave intimate descriptions of Carmel's Essene rituals when Mary, as a young child, was anointed by light as the one chosen from among the groups of twelve young maidens. Since Mary was identified as the chosen one when she was only four years of age, a decade or more passed before "the Annunciation." Although years passed, she was protected, groomed and trained at Carmel while the other candidates were allowed to go back to their homes to be married and bear children.

In eager anticipation, parents of the Essene community applied the name "Mary" to all hopeful girls; thus, most of them had a "spare name" provided for use after the "Chosen One" was singled out. This may explain why, according to the Cayce Readings, the Holy Mother had two sisters who were also named Mary. One, Elois (or Salome), married Zebedee, perhaps the richest man of Judea at the time as the owner of fleets of Mediterranean fishing vessels. The "other Mary" was Josie Mary, who was apparently much younger than Jesus' mother, although I have no idea by how many years, who was chosen while an infant to be second in line should the designated one fail to produce the Son of God.

As an honorable title, Josie Mary (#2946) grew up as "the Other Mary," probably even after Jesus was born and educated prior to baptism by his cousin, John. His ministry began when he was thirty. She married her nephew, Raoul, eldest son of her sister, Elois, and Zebedee. Cultural rules for marriage between relatives were different than ours today.

Raoul was the brother of Naomi, James and John, all of whom were first cousins of Jesus and, therefore, cousins, too, of John the Baptist. James and John became disciples of Jesus. The wedding was to be the most auspicious occasion for all the region. The guest list included other Essenes, of course, the Pharisees, and Sadducees, plus all the business associates of Zebedee. Invited, as well, were those highest ranking government officials who courted his favor. Being wealthy and gregarious, Zebedee was a powerful man, referred to as "Thunder." To attend the wedding celebration of his firstborn son was an opportunity of advantage sought by all, rich and poor, orthodox and unorthodox.

As a Bible reader, you were spared the details of such connections. Only the miracle of water being changed into wine at the wedding was featured in New Testament scriptures; whereas, the Cayce Readings provide all sorts of additional details that explain Jesus' Roman ties and the otherwise puzzling mix of the social register. Piecing together the many individual Readings, it is evident that Jesus, whose younger sister, Ruth (#1158), was later wed to Rome's top diplomat, Philoas (#1151), had no intention of overthrowing the political powers of their control. Jesus, in his role as the spiritual example of humanity's potential to identify with the divine core of Being, is paramount in Shepherding God's Flock for Heaven's Fold.

Background evaluation of Judea's history is reiterated in various Readings. Since John the Baptist's father, Zacharias, was the priest through whose tribal lineage, John rightfully should have assumed the position of High Priest in the Temple of Jerusalem. Killed by usurpers of that role prior to John's birth, the orthodox Jewish Temple rulers were no longer legitimate by Jewish heritage laws. King Herod, John's murderer, an arrogant egotist, being made aware of his potential replacement, used military guards to enforce control of the Temple, even by replacing Priests.

Already divided in factions adhering to different belief systems, the people chose to follow leaders among their ranks as Pharisees, Sadducees or Essenes. The Sanhedrin, a Parliamentarian sort of body, vied for religious control and paid tribute tithes to their physical King, Herod, while collecting fees for services to the poor, operational upkeep of their local synagogues and Jerusalem's temple. Herod's sons did likewise after his demise.

Occupied by the Romans, Judea's people were under control of a foreign Caesar whose empire demanded additional taxes. Rome allowed their own

Jewish king, Herod II at the time, full control of their religious rituals. Secular management by an appointed Governor, Pontius Pilate, acting as a judge with military forces to collect taxes and enforce behavioral conduct, linked them with other provinces of Caesar's vast empire. Herod II, as his father before him, was abusive by temperament and courted the favor of Rome's elite while using the Priesthood's lineage as his tool for political suppression.

Judea's allegiance was in total chaos. Occupied by foreign control and corrupt religious usurpers, the faithful could see little sign of hope as they struggled to survive during one of the worst periods of their volatile history. Anarchy loomed throughout their confused land. John, the Baptist, and Jesus, the Promised One, matured during the ensuing chaotic crisis.

Foremost among such spiritual impoverishment perpetrated by the Church centuries later was Empress Theodora's edict, enforced by evil collaborators whose tribes are prolific. Deception still cloaked the leaders of religions, and their sanctioned teachings evaded that fundamental Truth that souls return, again and again, to reincarnate, usurping power over their flocks in the guise of their roles of Church State Rulers.

The separation of Church and State rule has made it possible for many seekers to discover that enlightenment is awakened from within each soul by choice, rather than by edict. In many parts of the world today, associations of like-minded worshippers can now enhance their faith and joy in sharing understanding with each other, without fear of censure or reprisal from the State or misguided religious authorities.

Recognizing or praising God was never a part of America's founders restrictions by law; but forcing others to bow under specific religious interpretations was instilled as a definite no-no! Among their prized aims was that no religious group or tyrannical individual could usurp another's right to worship God as he/she saw fit.

Among America's first European settlers were dissidents of society, and religions, indentured servants bought and sold as laborers by those who paid off their debts, and some were individuals bought from African tribes while enroute. Slavery became an issue so controversial during the initial planning by America's founders. Its hangovers have plagued the nation, leaving scars that have not yet healed in the hearts and minds of its citizens.

The theory of Reincarnation was still absent from that era's consideration. Had I been privileged to seek answers from Mr. Cayce, I would have asked for an explanation of one specific memory of being a slave before The War Between The States (as called in the deep South). Years ago, while serving A.R.E. as a volunteer coordinator for members in my area, I welcomed a new member to a Search For God study group meeting in my home. Although both of us are presently Caucasians, we recognized each other at first sight as former slaves. An impromptu song and dance routine in Swahili, or some such foreign language, followed our cordial greetings, as she stepped inside. The regular S.F.G. members were already seated in the living room and witnessed our exhibit in disbelief that we had not choreographed its weird sounds and moves prior to the event.

When our detailed explanations of where, when and names poured from us simultaneously, verifying recognition as valid, they applauded. Our group was congenial and understanding, since our memories harmonized in our mutually accepted beliefs. During the "sixties," that kind of unusual concord qualified us as a rarity among prayer groups in Richmond, Virginia, south of the Mason-Dixon Line.

Readings on soul reasons for specific placements of opportunity and abilities are sprinkled with information. For instance, one states that each of us are subject to the necessary training through experiencing all five races. The five senses are developed within each race: white corresponds to vision, yellow to hearing, red to touch, brown to smell and black to taste. Likewise, each race carries the potential for negative or positive use of each sense in varying degrees.

In order to dispel bigotry, it seems to me that a book written on that subject might serve to enlighten souls on the distinctive value, in terms of soul-development, of lessons learned from the perspective of experiencing a life lived as a member of each race. A warning was given that tolerance of all different races must be mastered in order to evolve into an unconditional, Agape Love. For, if people only realized hatred of a specific human race guarantees one the necessity to enter that race for embodiment on a subsequent incarnation, the realization might alter attitudes. Thus, a slave owner who abuses his or her slave will surely repay the debt of such abuse through being subjected to the same cruel, harsh treatment as a slave. Debts come due or must be accounted as forgiven.

God's accountants assure justice, though it is not obvious that the balance is determined during the short span of one lifetime. That is the mystery revelation that requires eternal vision. "Now, we see darkly, but then, face to face, or more clearly," to paraphrase a well-known verse of scripture.

That is Karma, the law of cause and effect, plain and simple, taught in lessons of experience, "an eye for an eye" justification. Since the plan is a dynamic balancing factor of reincarnation, pay-back or revenge is fulfilled automatically by Universal Law, thereby negating mankind's "Judgment." "Vengeance is Mine," saith the Lord (Romans 12:19). If we learned that one lesson, most likely there would be no wars, or, less necessity for recycling souls through reincarnation. Even sexuality preferences, such as homosexual attractions, might be better understood if we remembered the reasoning for switches in our gender from one entry to the next.

Love and obedience of spiritual law's universal principles would have freed us from the gravity of our planetary karma. However, self-discernment of error is an important aspect of our learning experience, prompting repentance. Not by words is discernment evaluated, but by the fruits—deeds, actions, reactions—of one's spirit. The results of our attitudes and behaviors are imprinted as influences that become incorporated into our spiritual identity. "Considerosity" is the key. When my son was four years old, he created this word to sum up the fruits of the spirit, and I have never found an adequate substitute. Gladys liked it, too. But then, she had a knack for appreciating kids of all kinds, and their creativity.

Today, being no longer deprived of such knowledge about reincarnation as to how life works in the process of spiritual development, one can choose the wiser course in application of personal talents, to grow in educational degrees of behavioral accomplishments. Many barriers to the theory have not yet been removed from our schools of religion. When Edgar Cayce faced the psychic recognition, he had difficulty reconciling the theory with his religious training, as many others of us do. Overcoming doubts and fears of being sidetracked from God's purpose for his gifts, he found abundant Truth in the guidance he willingly shared with all seekers Providence provided.

Evidence that God has an infinite desire to portray knowledge through channels of inspiration which energize its intake with a capacity to expand and circulate through the whole system, resembles the elements of air, water, minerals and the spirit of Life, Itself. To know and be known is Universal Law.

God declared His Glory in the awesome beauty and power of His creations that all should be aware of His presence. From the toughest cover of an ancient turtle's shell to the downy softness of the bluebird's insulation, He declares the wonder of His concern in all creation. In all expressions, the flow of communication stimulates our attitude of gratitude as a necessary motivation to be reinvested toward renewal and increase.

As conduits of His Spirit, we must communicate Love in fulfilling our destiny of purpose. Such emissaries of His Kingdom accompanied our Master as human souls received initial counsel when the maps and architectural plans were first revealed. Edgar Cayce and Gladys Davis were leaders then, and have willingly returned repeatedly to update our awareness as our course winds ever through this school of learning.

Although the Life Readings were given to individuals as revelations of past activities or transcripts of academic courses, graded in degrees of progress or failures of the lessons as each student chose to utilize interests and potentials, a study of their coordinated collection gives us a historical perspective of humanity as a specie of evolution, or devolution, depending on one's thesis.

The key in understanding our purpose is to have a closer relationship to our Creator and our fellow man as reflections of Him.

Mr. Cayce and Miss Gladys were attuned to such a mission of Enlightenment. Their sacrifices expended toward its cause show the patience of our Creator as we stumble through our paces of learning to walk upright and in Gladness with each other.

Sweet Blooms of Memory

Edgar Cayce, in a letter to #440, eloquently wrote:

The violet that blooms unseen, or though its odor goes on the desert air, has not lost its reward in doing and being that which the First Cause, or God, intended it to do or be.

Among Gladys' most ardent fans, Jim Hayden's exceptional floral contributions for so many occasions enhanced our memories of outstanding celebrations. Expressing beauty with dignity and joy, his arrangements infused the atmosphere with Gladness by reawakening our gratitude for Nature's bounty. Whether the occasion marked a ceremony of welcome to the conference members of A.R.E. or the memorial services of graduates from our midst, his generous displays added sensitivity to shared events. As an avid student of the Readings, whose questions plied the depths of Gladys' interpretations, his frequent floral gifts to her also spoke volumes in their mutual appreciation of the Work.

Just as Edgar Cayce enjoyed the benefits of his physical labors in cultivating his gardens of fruits and vegetables, flowers blooming on his landscapes added joy to his family's surroundings. Gladys, too, treasured the bonus of their beauty's lift. Albert Turner, her first husband, applied his recognition of that floral appeal when he traded Wall Street's employment for the cultivation of flowers in her vicinity.

Jim's bouquets supplied food for her soul's delight in her latter decades, while Vic Reiffer kept her humor fertile through supplying a constant delivery of comedic insights to her mailbox. Shared by her associates, their contributions benefited the camaraderie among the multitudes of her friends.

Each year her birthday is remembered as some of us gather to commemorate the significance of her legacy. Marking number 95 in this year of 2011, twenty-five years since her departure, Jim, true to his considerate nature, delivered to our joint hostesses another of his masterpiece floral arrangements. It danced with vibrant color and artistry, a touch of "Sunshine's Gladness" as we shared fond memories of her presence in our lives.

When asked what types of flowers he enjoyed most bringing to Gladys, Jim gazed wistfully at photographs of her which were arranged on the table and said violets and paper whites were his favorites, the violets so delicate yet stately in rich, royal purple, and the paper whites so rich in fragrance and purity. You could see in his face the span of years since her passing had not diminished his fondness for her memory. He spoke of a gift he had given her of one of his paintings of a grouping of wood violets entitled *"13 Violets for Miss Gladys,"* pictured here as it hangs in a beautiful, serene bedroom decorated with violets as its theme, a cherished memento of Gladys' niece, Deborah Strole.

Jim also shared some of his stories of Gladys at that birthday luncheon. When he had first come to the Beach to visit the A.R.E. in 1976, he was intent on finding the meditation room where the Glad Helpers were meeting. Passing a woman coming up from the old Hospital Building's basement, he asked if the group's meeting was being held upstairs. She told him it was, and they continued in opposite directions. A few minutes later, he found the woman he'd spoken to had turned around and run up the stairs after him. She told him she'd just

1-21-81   "13 Violets for Miss Gladys"   Jim Hayden

remembered that the meeting area had been changed and gave him corrected directions. Her humble manner and conscientious solicitude for his finding his destination left him assuming he'd spoken to a kindly staff member, perhaps one of the cleaning ladies. It wasn't until some time later that he realized this was Gladys Davis Turner, Mr. Cayce's former secretary and life partner in the Work. No self important celebrity diva, he found her to be as warm and approachable as an old friend and as attentive to the needs and comfort of visitors to A.R.E. as she was to preserving and sharing the Readings.

Jim stayed at the Beach and treasured a friendship with Gladys that evolved over the ensuing years. He shared flower arrangements, paintings and his own chauffeur services when needed and was a frequent dinner guest at Gladys' home. On one occasion, Jim told us, when he was driving her from the airport, he asked her what the most surprising thing was she felt she'd learned from the Readings.

He said Gladys shook her head at that question, saying that was too difficult, there were so many unexpected things learned. But with a young man's determination, he persisted. Eventually she complied and gave thoughtful consideration. "The most surprising thing," she answered, "was how easily we fool ourselves."

Jim's last sharing was a dream he had during Gladys' final weeks, when illness had confined her to a hospital bed. He told us he was soaring above the earth with arms outstretched, and with an awed sense of recent encounter with the Archangel Michael. He felt free in his consciousness and free from the imprisonment of his body. He then saw the A.R.E. from high above and was aware that there was an invisible line running through it, from North to South, that he had to align perfectly with as he came down.

He came down and found himself all alone by the front desk on the first floor. The scene shifted and he saw that he was on the second floor looking at Gladys' desk, her workplace having also the aspect of an altar and an aura of worship, as it was draped in deep purple fabric. Seeing the scalloped edges of that purple fabric, he realized that Gladys was about to die.

He walked over, sat down in her chair and pulled up to her desk. He felt the enormity of responsibility that went with that seat and tremendous honor in being allowed to sit there. Looking into her desk, he saw that it was both dark and infinite, vast with divinity, far beyond his own vision. Then, looking from the desk to his left, he saw a curious long row of odd looking TV sets, with deep blue chairs in front.

It was years later, in reconsidering this dream, that he realized the TV sets were computer monitors, unknown to his conscious mind at the time as the personal computer was not yet a part of our lives. He has since thought about that dream's many meanings and feels that, with today's accessibility of the Readings online, and the enormous research potential of the computer, we are all in a position of both honoring and carrying on Gladys' work. He sees that the future of our world may depend on the dedication of those who choose to use these resources for the ideal of service to one another which Gladys so exemplified.

In summary, Jim expressed his belief that there has been no entity in the earth who, like Jesus, worked with such goodness for the uplift of mankind. That what she did, in recording, copying and preserving these Readings is, even today, of untold benefit. We have yet to realize their full potential as he marvels at the unexpected gift of Gladys' friendship in his life.

Motivational Memories May Activate Yours

A recurring nightmare as a child, infused with the processing of images that alerted my interests as I listened to Bible stories being recounted, whether by ministers, Sunday School teachers, parents, or recollections of my own prolific memories, plagued me. The scene always began at the same place for me—Jerusalem.

There was a crowd of people, shoving each other along on a cobblestone street. The noise was a deafening mix of wails and jeers, moans and groans, laughing, crying. The clanking of metallic armor, stomping boots and clacking sandals rumbled the procession along. Stone walls on either side echoed the screaming curses, chants and murmured prayers in a babble of diverse languages, vibrating in chaotic disharmony.

The stench of frightened, angry, sweaty men, weeping women, wailing infants and young children was thick with dust, smoke and incense from the vendors' stalls. Swarming gnats and flies, having fed on the putrid garbage and dung that squished underfoot, dashed in droves to blight the eyes and nostrils of the multi-ethnic array of unwashed faces.

I studied those faces, some sobbing in uncontrollable agony, others stoic with clenched teeth, some spitting toward the soldiers or their prisoners. Groups of them were singing in animated celebration. Tired faces, old, young, bearded and beardless, grim ones and grinning ones, altogether expressing a grimy mosaic of humanity's total conglomeration.

Churned by the impact of raw emotions that shuffled the masses of packed bodies, I squirmed through the crevices. At last, I glimpsed the passing parade of soldiers. I could see one of their prisoners, the Galilean man whose red-gold hair I had heard the elders describe long before I had come to recognize it for myself. Wrapped around his head was a thick vine of long sharp thorns from which drools of blood rolled down his angular chiseled face. His eyebrows diverted pathways around the eyes to cruise along his battered nose, and alternate routes wound from the temples across his swollen bruised cheeks. Ruby beads sparkled randomly on His shoulder-length hair.

And then, as though the space between us shrank so that I felt near enough to touch his battered body, our eyes met in familiar salutation. He smiled, and I was somehow comforted, though my own eyes were blurred with tears. I squeezed them shut, as I sensed Love's presence within my soul. The crowd shifted me aside. Once more, I scanned the faces of the boisterous crowd and, in my bewilderment, *I SAW THAT EVERY FACE WAS MINE.*

Always awakening in a hyperventilating state, I found it difficult to sort my own reality in consciousness. Forced to arise, to console myself that I was blessed with health and comfortable environs, my thoughts would shift toward efforts of finding some perspective through analyzing the meaning of such an experience. Piecing other scenes that haunted my dreams from that same era, I sensed reincarnation, yet was denied the theory through our cultural heritage. As an avid participant in the church of my parents, and theirs, I was allowed to lead in prayer and teaching classes by the age of ten. When called upon to "talk" on a Palm Sunday to the class that included my dad and granddad, by their regular teacher, I didn't hesitate.

They got the whole nine yards, stuff the Holy Bible authors did not divulge, or if so, found deleted by its publishers. An elders fan club was initiated then and there, and the series of my "talks" became requested often, since my "imagination" seemed limitless to them. I brazenly gave answers to their questions that fascinated their search for inspiration, or entertainment, I don't know which.

It was not until I joined the followers of Edgar Cayce that I found parallel insertions of the stories that my limitless imagination had found so comforting to entertain. When I was introduced to the faces I recognized from those ancient encounters, I felt that I had found my real family.

There are certain aspects among the traits of many members that I find at odds with those I felt so closely associated with in former lifetimes. I am not sure how to reconcile what I see as alien behaviors, preferring to see the flaws as my own alterations in visual reflections. As someone long ago expressed it, we could not recognize the character flaws in others if we have not experienced them in ourselves. "It takes one to know one."

There's an incident that probably shows my true colors as well as any, in my attempt to be honest. Believe me, I have never been allowed to evade my shortcomings as I so quickly identify everyone else's motes. The beams in my own sockets are giant redwoods, for which I accept full responsibility in shame. This is a typical example of origin in my escapades.

I was blessed with the opportunity to travel in the Holy Lands of the Middle East, having yearned a lifetime to do so. The entire journey was filled with fantastic adventures as I *"de ja vu-ed"* each tourist-trap along the route, and a few bonus adventures that elude many by sharing time with friends like Mark Lehner while he was a student in Egypt, Ahmed Fayed's Pyramid family and Dr. and Mrs. Thor Hyerdahl, as they were creating their Museum on the Nile.

When I arrived at the phenomenal ruins site of Baalbek, vendors approached as we stepped off the tour bus, which is par for any tourist course. A rather persistent young man dogged my steps as I tried to soak in the overwhelming magnitude of the archeological structures. He kept working to get my attention of his wares. Holding out three coins that were "found on this ancient site," he insisted that I look at them, feel them, see how authentic they were. I took them, looked, felt and was duly impressed, but gave them back to him with my usual "procrastination" promise, that I would think about it, but did not wish to add any luggage until shortly before boarding the bus to leave the premises. I was eager to see the site itself. Eventually, he realized that I meant what I said and set his energies in pursuit of other potential clients.

Throughout the long, hot day, I found his activities to be an interesting distraction. Over and over, our paths crossed and I observed the pattern of his sales pitch. The open palm cradled three coins for observation as he

charmed each tourist with his slightly accented English, baptized in New York's colloquialisms, "Five bucks fah de whole schmeer!" His black eyes sparkled as his smile magnetically seduced each customer who dutifully searched through their billfold to produce the signaled response. As he retrieved the coins, he produced a small paper envelope, appeared to drop the tinkling coins into it, sealed its top and made the exchange of his gift

for their bill. Pleasantries exchanged as each parted wearing his own smile. I found it fascinating that each time I next viewed the contents appearing on his open hand, duplicates of the original coins seemed to appear.

When our bus driver parked in the spot designated for our group to reload for departure, I headed for its welcome cushioned seats. Stones had lined the walkways, and benches of stone allowed us to rest our weary feet. The eyes could locate little other color in their sweep of sand and layered columns of palatial structures than the dwarfed figures clad in tourists garbs. Even the sparse vegetation took on the neutrality of its dust. The broiling sun seemed to shrink the lengths and depths of shadows that offered temporary refuges in the great expanse of structures, as I remember that day.

Eager to locate a seat on the bus, I greeted the driver as a familiar friend. He stood by its open door, as I started up its steps. A hand on my shoulder tugged, as a breathless vendor interrupted my ascent. "Wait. You promised to buy my coins." I stepped aside to let others enter the bus. His patterned pitch began as the bus driver looked on. He knew the vendor, I felt sure, since both frequented the area in pursuing their respective occupations. I checked the coins quite thoroughly, feeling satisfied that they were as authentic as could be, and I knew that they were the originals that I had held when we arrived at the site.

I pondered the dilemma, as the bus filled and I asked the driver if everyone was on board but me. He nodded. I gave him a wink as I stepped closer to the open bus door. Handing the vendor a folded fiver, I dropped the coins into my open purse as I ascended the steps. The bus driver followed me, as he pulled the door swiftly behind him. Having been foiled in his plot, the vendor screamed as he beat his fist on the heavy window of the door, and on the side of the bus as the driver started its engine and moved out as soon as I was seated. Turning his torso to look in my direction, he laughed heartily as our eyes met. Doffing his cap in a grand salute, he showed his approval of the coup I had just accomplished.

The bus moved forward as the angry vendor followed, screaming in his native tongue, tears streaking his dusty face. As my fellow travelers questioned the meaning of what they had witnessed, I let the driver do the explanations, finding my sensitivity for the vendor's loss too painful for gloating.

Since a number of them had bought his shtick, they began investigating their sealed collections. Finding slugs that barely resembled coins, they began to send negative vibes in his direction as they thanked me for giving him a just revenge, I said, "Wait a minute, the guy is trying to make a living in one of the poorest areas of the world. You knew that if you were buying ancient coins, five bucks would have been highway robbery, which is what I did to him. So, in his assuming that, as rich Americans affording travel to his homeland, 'What is a small fee for entertaining you with a little slight of hand magic, that can feed my family?' You won't miss it, see?"

My conscience as my brother's keeper is not so clear as to my own motive. I want to think I was helping him learn honesty, but was I being greedy, or sanctimonious?

When I had an appraisal of the coins made years later, I learned that my initial impression was correct and verified my own selfish urge to claim one as a keepsake. The largest one, with the head of King Croesus II, dates back to the time of the City of the Hills and the Plains, when Gladys and I were friends thousands of years ago. The coin, interesting as a sunburst symbol, is for me a reminder of our relationship that goes so far back. "Sunshine," as her apt nickname reminds me with this coin, is worn as a special amulet body pendant symbolizing that period of her favorite lifetime. She got a kick

190

out of my use of it as a reminder of our relationship and was amused by the intrigue of my acquisition. Since banditry was such a part of that Persian period of our shared lifetime, it seemed apropos to me, but I dared not ask what she may have thought of my roguishness.

Evidently, while I retained the cultural stigma of that pattern, Gladys found it almost impossible to see deceit in other human beings. Her attunement to the higher calling of magnifying the ideal with such brilliance that shadows of unrighteous behavior could barely cloud the potential she focused on, as she shared contact with us. Her faith held that as we grew in awareness our old habits would be discarded and replaced with desires for a more positive approach under the Law of Grace. She ignored the flaws as temporary impediments unworthy of blocking the tides of change that would move us forward.

In minimizing faults, Love forced her to maximize the positive potential she trusted implicitly would eventually redeem us from error. Love nurtures such patience while multiplying itself. And to think, I considered her "naive" because she could not discern the shallowness of male chauvinists. How much I have yet to learn!

Her open honesty permitted no sanctuaries of defensive evasion of behavioral traits, as expressed by herself especially. She was candidly capable of observing her own education through the benefits of mentors, whether contacts drawn as participants or Readings of advice to others or for herself. Her vast tolerance, understanding and sincerity of applying gems of wisdom as tools of self-improvement was an anomaly. Childlike in her unabashed desire to learn, she therefore epitomized the teacher. Having cared for her in Egypt, I found my memory of the "perfect child" hard to erase, even as I shared her mature friendship.

Jesus said in Matthew 18:3-4 that unless we become as little children we cannot enter heaven. "Whosoever therefore shall humble himself as this little child, the same is greatest in the kingdom of heaven."

Her "hope" was never anchored to human practicality, but soared by angelic propulsion. Its three-fold nature—prayer, meditation and dream revelation—all facets of the same oneness with the God forces she activated daily. Memories of her inspirational example of virtue levitates my spirit in aspiring to follow in that "Sunshine of Gladness!"

My Memory Adjustments of Jesus' Lifetime

If there are traces of memory here with which your soul resonates, then you can imagine the way I have relived the details of events that surrounded the experiences of that period in ancient history by which the world calculates time. Born into humanity's chaos, aware of His potential fate, knowing that in using free will, He had the power to effect its outcome. Yet, none of Jesus' fellow souls could appreciate the full weight of His perceived determination. Even after thousands of years, billions of individuals have yet to reach a consensus of the merits of His sacrifice in behalf of God's children. As brothers and sisters we have not yet recognized our spiritual source of Oneness in kinship. So engrossed in satisfying self's appetites, few of us bother to be concerned about the Source of our supply, only that we claim our share of it by any means available with little regard for the consequences!

Imagine the struggle of His most momentous decision: "To be, or not to be" the sacrificial lamb? Since volunteering for the mission, His spirit, willing to endure the potter's wheel as Adam and the subsequent incarnations in experiencing all the trials and tribulations that humanity faces, celebrated as Love triumphed through each. As Jesus, His most excruciating test loomed.

The final decision was one of absolute surrender to the agonies He knew in full anticipation. Commitment, with no reservations, required a price no other human could calculate. The years of effort expended in training groups through history and in every geographical area of the planet had reached the peak of preparation for the final test of free will. The covenant, to prove God's undeniable Love of every soul that fulfills its spiritual potential, was at stake in this execution. No wonder the stress turned His perspiration to beads of blood in that trial of surrender to the Will of Our Mutual Source of Eternal Life. Having agreed to allow the outcome to be controlled by God's Love, He faced the physical and mental endurance tests of the crucifixion with resignation and absolute obedience to God's Will.

Knowing the variety of experiences in human form had run the gamut of consequences of trials and lessons to be learned, His final test would determine the fate of mankind in its role in spiritual eternity. Having so lived that none dare question God's Love concerning all fellow beings if they conduct their free will choices by the pattern He set, His trust was sufficient to face and endure opposition of the world's fury. In recognizing Hate as ignorance of Love's power, He pleaded for our forgiveness, that Light might dissipate the pestilential shadows recessed in our selfish wills.

For the family, friends and followers who loved Him, the injustice of His prosecution was almost unbearable, and, although He had forewarned with incomprehensible words, none of us could imagine that such a mockery of Justice could occur. Our understanding was vacant, our violent emotions rampant. Throughout the preceding week, from His jubilant entry into the overcrowded city of celebrants, uncontrollable eruptions had mounted into a chaotic mix of joy, despair, love, hate, anxiety and hope.

Political fervor rose among the citizens whose intolerance of foreign rule, corrupt decline in religious and secular leadership, and rising criminal elements in every nook and cranny had reached its zenith. False prophets were everywhere. Jesus and His disciples had brought hope with its cautionary belief that anyone could fix Jerusalem's challenges. Today's generation can surely identify with their predicament, even these millennia since, as the chaos of today parallels such various frustrating disasters. Emotions operate reactions, blurring civil controls. True fruits of spiritual development are recognizably sparse.

Edgar Cayce's references were expansive in covering that period of history, through many clients' Readings describing details of their experiences there, during and after Jesus' Crucifixion and Resurrection. Collation of excerpts gleaned from the many individuals sharing that era maps a scenario that defies many concepts which former scholars have concluded. Alterations of long-held beliefs in religious history are as controversial as adapting new scientific theories. Vested interests are not limited to just ideas, but in established organizations, rooted in powers controlling political hierarchies of many denominations and the economics of all. Such worldly alterations precludes even the Theological consideration of such conceptual pro-portions. Patience must persist for Peace to exist.

Bridging the relationships of Jesus' adoring family, friends and devoted followers while His associates included ruling forces of Rome, Herod's Court, Pharisees, Sadducees, Essenes, rich, poor, Jews, Gentiles, believers, non-believers, sinners and saints, Mr. Cayce gave samples of their complex residual imprints affecting twentieth century survivors. As one of the seventy young men chosen by Jesus to recruit believers and later appointed as

193

Bishop of Laodicea, the headquarters of early Christians, Edgar Cayce knew first-hand the challenges faced by generations following the Resurrection and the deciphering of our spiritual legacy.

As a mother whose son was healed by the Master, and as a close friend of Ruth, Jesus' sister during that lifetime, I treasure the memories of our personal friendships then and again in the present. The agonies from watching the angry mobs demanding His execution haunt my dreams. Centuries later, pondering behavioral understanding of fellow citizens whose concepts differ from my own assessments of politics and prose ensues. Justifiable anger, no doubt, has its merit, but learning to apply Love's power of perspective reasoning with such adversaries still tests the depths of accumulated wisdom at eighty-five years of age.

Knowing that Pilate was a friend of Philoas, the brother-in-law of Jesus, as well as Caesar's chosen ambassador and, therefore, Pilate's superior, I believed that he would protect Jesus from the unruly mob. Philoas was not yet back from an official trip to Rome, which is possibly why Ananias and his son-in-law, Caiphas, had been able to convince Herod that it was an ideal time to capture Jesus as prisoner. Their cunning ploy worked, as Jesus intuitively had anticipated. Previously, there had been attempts to detain Jesus when he had phenomenally eluded their grasp, as Pilate and Jesus' followers well knew.

Roman expansion had flexed its military might to dominate the Mediterranean circumference by controlling their subjects with its inference of fear. However, the Caesars ruled their provinces with intellect that bargained amply in exchanges of services that appealed to their masses in as peaceful solutions as possible. Sharing the Greco-Roman Gods and socio-economic benefits, the military powers were generally fused in a united method of control over the regions cultures. Israel's historical heritage was exceptional because of its Religion. Since its adherents had so consistently fought for perseverance of their worship of The One God as dearer than survival of life, wars had been so extremely bloody for its conquerors and enslavement of their remnant survivors was the only option when over-coming their territory.

Rome made exceptions for Judea's province. Since Herod (the Tetrarch) found Roman lifestyle most appealing, he had embraced its tastes of debauchery and outright war was averted in the negotiations so that their religion was left intact under Herod's control. His gross indulgence in sensual appetites had seduced all virtue, duty and fidelity to the dictates of his religious ancestors, no longer following the disciplines of their heritage as he aligned with Roman rule.

When Zacharias, father of John the Baptist, was murdered as he clung to the Temple altar, Herod dared to replace the priesthood lineage with his political proteges, knowing that his royal guardsmen could use the Roman army as a force to quell riots of religious adherents. Thirty years later, the religious masses had split into volatile factions among the Pharisees, Sadducees, Essenes and scattered extremists opposing all with whom they disagreed. Undercurrents of frustration and disharmony permeated every section of Judea's citizenry. Confusion in whom or what to believe reigned in utter chaos of uncontrollable despair. Hope and faith in deliverance from oppression seemed impossible as tolerance waned.

New Testament scholars find details sparse in identifying key players and events of that historical period, as records were either unwritten then, or destroyed later, in acquiescence of survival. Thus Cayce's Akashic interpretations stand out as barely supported, except by the memories of the few whose recall paralleled his Readings or trusted the uncanny phenomena of his adherence to Truth. Church historians have been lax in disseminating reliable information to adequately explain the glaring gaps in the selected Biblical literature. So, I am sharing the details from recall in hopes of a more comprehensive appreciation of the community of Jesus' associates, whose contacts have continued to enlarge my understanding of this mission He initiated in behalf of God's Glory and our fellow spiritual seekers. Having been given their permission to identify them by names, then and in this century, where applicable, I will give their reading numbers so that you may further study their lives if you choose.

Ruth, #1158, and Philoas, #1151, (Irene and Milton Harrison) as Jesus' sister and brother-in-law, chose to live in Caesarea after their marriage ceremony, officiated by Jesus as a young Rabbi following the wedding of Zebedee's eldest son and their mother's youngest sister, when the water had been changed to wine. Although Philoas' role with Tiberius ranked him as overseer of the Governors of Mediterranean provinces, he became personally aware of the circle of Jesus' associates, business and religious leaders, tax gatherers and concerns of Judea's ordinary citizens. He and

Jesus shared mutual family concerns and visits, as did Pilate's family, because of their mutual palatial residence proximity. Because of the friendship ties within the small country of strong family bonds, Jesus was not a stranger to those in each echelon of authority. Linkage of their connections to each other tied families of diverse ethnic, trade and heritage backgrounds, tracing a web-like pattern of communication throughout Judea. Their "Internet" spread the news across the towns and rural areas, affecting friends and foes with anxious repercussions in a remarkable speed, before our technologically advanced era.

Nicodemus (#3031), a leader among Pharisees, had wed a young Essene woman, Martha (#3175), Ruth Burks. Her mother, Sophia, was a close friend of Judy (#1472), and her older sister, Esdrella (#1541), was Peter's mother-in-law. Martha wove "the robe" Jesus wore, for which the soldiers cast lots, as a one-piece garment, in gratitude for the healing of her sister and also a nephew of Nicodemus. Active in Jerusalem's Temple as his dutiful wife, her ties with her sister, Esdrella, and their mother bridged connections with the Disciples and Judy's fellow Carmel leaders with activities at the Temple of Jerusalem. As Nicodemus' wife, again, in the twentieth century, Ruth's re-encounter with Edgar Cayce was a renewal of recognition for both. I met her through Mildred Davis (#295) and shared visits with both in her home.

When Nicodemus had asked Jesus how he might get to Paradise, the answer was that he must be born again, so in the nineteenth century he made it to Paradise, Pennsylvania, where he lived and died. I find it interesting, too, that Mildred Davis, as the reincarnation of Mary Magdalene, had been a resident of Bethany, OK. Jesus often visited Lazarus, Martha and Mary in Biblical Bethany. Visiting her daughter, Elaine, in her eighty-fifth year of life, she died there on November 14, 1987. Her grave lies next to her husband's in Oklahoma City.

Along the way, errors found by staff member recorders of A.R.E. needed to be corrected, occasionally. Even Gladys corrected errors in reports that she discovered years after their first printing. An example was that Clana, daughter of Cleopas, was the bride at Cana, as later corrected was that Josie Mary was Bride, and Clana, her "Maid of Honor." No big deal, but genealogists of that period have a tough challenge sorting the "begats." For as researchers adapted the initial account into their writings, it helped to scatter the error before the retraction was made available. Unintended faults are possible, when done in translations of Biblical scripture, adding chaos to interpretations and misunderstandings between debaters of presumed facts. So, "What is Truth, really?" Edgar Cayce gave a great lecture on the subject at a conference held during the Cayce Hospital days. It is included in a report #1800-15.

In contemplating the complex state of today's world, I realize that my views differ radically from the perceptions of the general population. And precisely because my insights are so atypical, it follows then that my conclusions range far from those of many, if not most, of my contemporaries. But during my lifetime, I have recognized with "Gladitude" the precepts gleaned from my association with the Edgar Cayce Readings and Gladys have brought great comfort and clarity in seeking God's purpose in my own life.

In Closing

Gladys trusted Edgar Cayce's translation of God's message as absolute, believing God had chosen him to deliver it. Doubting God was not possible since she, too, had been chosen by Him for her role in the same vital mission. Would that the rest of us were so wise and free of doubts and fears to block our Faith. When quoting God's messengers, she knew that no ordinary human being was intelligent enough to improve on God's chosen words. Her duty, as she followed her well-developed intuition, was to respect His words as profound Truth, not to be trifled with for individual clarification.

Her tenacity and reverent connection, irrespective of multiple talents, would have proven useless without the qualities that she possessed to dedicate herself to the cause, her sense of purpose in expressing each breath of life force inspiration as tools designed to aid others. Finding their connection to Goodness, as Gladness that their endowment as natives with allegiance to the Source of All Supply increased their bounty of talents as they shared gratitude through services to fellow natives, fulfilled her mission as it also extended the benefits of Edgar Cayce's life purpose. In total agreement with the prescriptions God wrote while Cayce translated, she proved the merits of their ingredients by incorporating and living accordingly as an example for others to emulate. Her mantra was always "Others." Our acclaim for her is, "Well done, God's good and faithful servant!"

I wrote the following poem using sensory tools of recognition during Gladys' life as I "Re-Encountered" many souls from my Persian and Judean lifetimes.

We Meet Again

Your voice recalls the sounds of Heaven's chorus
Of realms on mystic planes beyond the stars,
Like whisp'ring windsongs during summer showers,
While harpists symphonize vibrations' happy hours,
Of Sunny rings from Saturn, Jupiter, Uranus, even Mars,
Notes of harmony with Pluto, Mercury, and Neptune,
Replaying psalms of lovely Venus dancing with our Moon.
Your eyes excite emotions as the seas that wash ashore
Move sands of time, long-pillowed in the memories of more
Elusive moments. Treasured relics, eons-covered
'Neath the waves of lifespans' lore,
Lifts to surface mirrored glimpse of
Ancient roles we shared before.
Your face reflects familiar friendships,
Reminiscent scenes of yore,
Beaming warmth of joy in being
Brought together thus, once more.
Slightly scarred by past encounters,
Veiled in dreamy poignant plots
The yens evade full revelations,
Yet sways the logic of my conscious thoughts.
Your hands uncover glowing embers
From the fires of Yesterday,
Souvenirs of warm vibrations
Spark to flame again today.
Like sunbeams through the clouded mists
Bring rainbows into view
Your touch creates the golden threads
That weave soul memories with you.
Thus our re-encounter wakens
Haunting themes of music's flow
From the Source of Inspiration,
Bringing forth desire to know
More of purpose, sense of progress.
Recognition through recall
Of the lessons learned as students
Through each lifetime, lest we fall,
While building bridges from this Earth plane
Arched toward Heaven, saving All.

How blessed I feel to have witnessed the courage Gladys shared in leading through service, enlightening the way as she carried the banner of cooperation. For our generation, and those who follow, I have found no greater shining example than the beacon shown in her life as REFLECTIONS OF GLADNESS!

Until we meet again, my heart sings these verses in Gladitude:

> From the gossamer strands of friendship's web,
> Your memory weaves perceptive traces
> Where "Sunshine's" kiss upon Earth's sands,
> Left warm rays' tingling
> To stir our better understanding
> Of the paths we've trod together,
> Along life's shores we share forever.

Micki and Gladys

MAY GOD BLESS YOU!

Wired by Nature to use its electrical force, our Creator allows each soul to choose the appliances available to design its own destiny.

Characterized as Love or Hate (or from Light or Dark Forces), we are presented with the tools of choice by which we fashion the patterns of our existence on this plane. Services for Good or Evil shape our results as we use our mind and heart's control to follow or ignore the examples and signs set as guides.

Reincarnation is one theory among many. Its focus enlists a belief in repeated opportunities for alterations through the school of experience, as designed by God's Grace and Patience for training His spiritual children to be ideal expressions of Eternal Love.

By acquiring this book, you have added to the potential of the Association of Research and Enlightenment to expand the Work as pioneered by Edgar Cayce and Gladys Davis, through your gift to:

The Gladys Davis Endowment Fund
Initiated in honor of her exemplary service,
to be an ideal pattern for followers who desire to
expand similar concerns being shared by a
World of Glad Helpers.
Thank You!

For information, please contact info@reflectionsofgladness.com.

ABOUT THE AUTHOR

Micki Kluge, artist and author, lives in Virginia Beach, Virginia, and has been a student of the Edgar Cayce Readings for many years. She shares memories of her friend, Gladys Davis, along with remembrances of friends and family who cherished her.